PhotoPlus 11 User Guide

GW00319961

How to contact us

Our main office (UK, Europe):

The Software Centre
PO Box 2000, Nottingham, NG11 7GW, UK

Main	(0115) 914 2000
Registration (UK only)	(0800) 376 1989
Sales (UK only)	(0800) 376 7070
Technical Support (UK only)	(0845) 345 6770
Customer Service (UK only)	(0845) 345 6770
Customer Service/	
Technical Support (International)	+44 115 914 9090
General Fax	(0115) 914 2020
Technical Support email	support@serif.co.uk

American office (USA, Canada):

The Software Centre
13 Columbia Drive, Suite 5, Amherst, NH 03031

Main	(603) 889-8650
Registration	(800) 794-6876
Sales	(800) 55-SERIF or 557-3743
Technical Support	(603) 886-6642
Customer Service	(800) 489-6720
General Fax	(603) 889-1127
Technical Support email	support@serif.com

Online

Visit us on the Web at	http://www.serif.com
Serif newsgroups	news://news.serif.com

International

Please contact your local distributor/dealer. For further details please contact us at one of our phone numbers above.

Comments or other feedback

We want to hear from you! Please email feedback@serif.com with your ideas and comments!

Contents

1.   Welcome   1

Introduction 3
About the User Guide 3
What's New in PhotoPlus 11.. 4
   New Features 4
   Power.. 5
   Ease of Use 6
Established Features 7
Registration, Upgrades, and Support 12
Installation... 12
   System requirements.. 12
   First-time install.. 13
   Manual install/re-install 13

2.   Getting Started   15

Seven Key Concepts 17
   1 Image size and canvas size 17
   2 Interacting tools and tabs 17
   3 Making a selection.. 18
   4 Foreground and background colours 18
   5 Layers.. 18
   6 Opacity and transparency...................................... 19
   7 Saving and exporting.. 20
Starting PhotoPlus 21
Getting Your Bearings.. 22
   Introducing the interface 23
   Principal PhotoPlus Toolbars and Tabs 24
   Managing Workspace Tabs... 28
   Context toolbars.. 29
   Setting preferences 29
   Setting the view 29
How to Get an Image into PhotoPlus.............................. 30
   Screen Capture.. 32
Saving and Exporting Files 34

Print Output 36

Sharing documents by email 37

Setting the file type 37

Setting your image size 37

3.   Manipulating Images   39

Making Selections 41

Selection options 41

Modifying the selection 45

Variable selections 47

Using the Move Tool 48

Cut, Copy, Paste, Delete 49

Cropping 49

Flipping, Rotating, and Deforming 50

Using Mesh Warp 52

Channels 54

Adjusting Image Values 56

Adjustment layers 58

Adjusting brightness and contrast 59

Correcting Images 60

Using the Retouch tools 60

Using QuickFix Studio 62

Applying Special Effects 65

Using Effect Filters 65

Using the Filter Gallery 65

Instant Artist Effects 67

2D/3D Effects 68

Tutorial Resources 69

4.   Working with Paint, Shapes, and Text   71

Choosing Colours 73

Painting and Drawing 75

Using the basic Paintbrush Tool 75

Choosing and customizing brush tips 76

Context toolbar 77

Brush characteristics 79

Painting with a pattern 80
Using the Picture Brush tool 81
Using the Eraser tools 82
Warping and Cloning 83
Using the Warp tools 83
Using the Clone Tool 84
Creating and Editing Lines and Shapes 85
QuickShapes 87
Outline shapes.. 88
Editing shapes 89
Filling Regions... 90
Flood and pattern fills 91
Gradient fills... 92
Editing a gradient fill 94
Working with Paths 95
Working with Text 98
Text Selections 99
Tutorial Resources... 100

5. Using Layers and Masks 101

Layers 103
Kinds of layers 103
Basic layer operations 105
Manipulating layers.. 106
Selecting layers 106
Moving the contents of one or more layers 107
Linking layers.. 107
Aligning layers 107
Deleting Layers.. 108
Clipboard operations involving layers......................... 108
Rearranging layers in the stack................................. 108
Merging layers 109
Grouping Layers 109
Blend Modes... 110
Blend Ranges 111
Extracting part of a layer.. 112
Layer Effects.. 112
Depth Maps 115

Masks 117
  Mask-making 117
  1 Creating the Mask 118
  2 Editing on the Mask 119
  3 Applying changes to the layer 120
  Tutorial Resources 121

6.   Preparing Web Graphics   123

Formats for the Web 125
  .GIF format 125
  .JPG format 126
  .PNG format 126
Producing Web Animations 128
  Layers and frames 128
  Notes on animation 131
  Animation effects 132
Image Slicing 132
  Slicing an image 133
Image Maps 133
  Creating hotspots 134

7.   Macros and Batch Processing   137

Understanding Macros 139
  Recording a Macro 140
  Playing a Macro 141
  Modifying a Macro 141
Batch Processing 143
  Using Macros 143
  Changing File Type 144
  Choosing Source and Destination 144
Tutorial Resources 145

8.   Colour and Input/Output Options   147

Colour Concepts 149
  Bitmaps 149
  Bit depth 149

Bit depth in PhotoPlus 150
Resolution... 151
Colour modes 151
Colour matching... 153
Colour mode tips... 153
Using the Histogram 154
Viewing statistics 154
Optimizing Images 155
Palettes.. 156
Dithering 157
Compression.. 157
File Formats... 158
Tips for Scanning 158
EXIF Information 160
Advanced Printing... 161
Positioning, scaling, and tiling 161
CMYK colour separations... 162
Including printer marks 162
Multi-Image Printing 164
Publishing a PDF File 164
Tutorial Resources.. 166
PhotoPlus Keyboard Shortcuts.. 167
Tool shortcuts 167
Menu command shortcuts 168

9.   Index   171

Contents

Welcome

Introduction

Welcome to Serif PhotoPlus 11—a fantastic photo-editing solution ideal for any home, school, organization, or growing business. PhotoPlus is your number one choice for working with photographs and paint-type images, whether for the Web, multimedia, or the printed page.

PhotoPlus has the features you'll need... from importing or creating pictures, through manipulating colours, making image adjustments, applying effects (filter, 2D and 3D) and so much more, all the way to final export. Built-in support for TWAIN cameras (and scanners) makes it easy to bring in your very own digital photos, while comprehensive import filters let you open just about any standard bitmap image.

About the User Guide

This User Guide is your guide to getting started and getting results with PhotoPlus—from the basics to advanced techniques. The chapter sequence begins with basic concepts and proceeds gradually through various tools and features. Here's a quick summary of chapter contents:

1. **Welcome.** An introduction to PhotoPlus, with new and established feature lists.

2. **Getting Started.** Will have you up and running in no time with an overview of key concepts and the PhotoPlus interface.

3. **Manipulating Images.** A rundown of basic techniques for selecting and operating on all or just part of an image, including application of photo-correction and special effect filters.

4. **Working with Paint, Shapes, and Text.** How to proceed from the proverbial blank slate, using the PhotoPlus creation tools.

5. **Using Layers and Masks.** Understanding and mastering the creative possibilities of these more advanced features.

6. **Preparing Web Graphics.** A review of Web image formats and step-by-step guidance on animation and image preparation.

7. **Macros and Batch Processing.** Automate your PhotoPlus actions to increase your efficiency.

8. **Colour and Input/Output Options.** Combines essential background material and terminology with helpful tips to improve your images.

9. **Index.** Use for quick access to the information you need!

What's New in PhotoPlus 11

Whether you're a new or returning PhotoPlus user, take some time out to review the following new features available in PhotoPlus 11:

New Features

- **QuickFix Studio— for one-stop image adjustments** (p. 62)
  Use the QuickFix Studio environment to make cumulative image adjustments to **Brightness&Contrast** and **Colour**, as well as **Straighten** and **Crop** your images. Equally apply **Greyscale**, **Sharpen**, and fix **Red Eye** plus **Lens Distortion**, **Lens Vignette** and **Chromatic Aberration** (see below). A full-screen dual-image preview display lets you compare and fix your images in an instant.

- **Filters—correct image distortion and more!** (p. 63)
  Apply **Lens Distortion** to fix barrel or pincushion distortion, **Lens Vignette** to remove darkening at the edges of an image and **Chromatic Aberration Remover** to remove coloured haloing around bright objects. The **Lens Filter** image adjustment lets you "warm up" or "cool down" any photo. More **creative filters** include a **Depth of Field** blur (apply as a linear or radial gradient, or to a layer mask) and an **Average Colour** filter (fills selection with average colour of the selected area). Last but not least.. use **Matisse**-style **Paper Cutouts** to simulate collages of multi-coloured paper.

- **Photo Studio toolbar** (p. 24)
  Access the new QuickFix Studio, along with Filter Gallery, Instant Artist, and the Extract tool with this new toolbar, handily placed above your workspace.

- **New version—New tools!**
  Already packed full of Photo-editing tools, PhotoPlus now supports even more! The **Pencil Tool** (for pixel-level editing and hard-edged brush work), **Selection Deform Tool** (for changing a selection's shape), **Replace Colour Tool** (for painting foreground colours over background colours) and **Straighten Tool** (for re-aligning a crooked photo prior to cropping) are all exciting additions.

- **Crop to common print sizes** (p. 49)
  Use the **Crop Tool** for easy cropping to commonly used portrait and landscape print sizes (4 x 6 in, 5 x 7 in, 6 x 4 in, 7 x 5 in, etc.)—print resolution will auto-adjust to honour any print size. Even use a **Custom** crop size to produce photos with non-standard dimensions.

- **Screen Capture** (p. 32)
  Perform screen captures of your **Active Window, Client Area, Full Screen, Selected Object**, or **Selected Area**. Delay timer, hot key support, and cursor inclusion options contribute to make this a powerful and creative tool within PhotoPlus.

- **More Tabs to support photo-editing** (p. 24)
  Store frequently used colours (e.g. during retouching) in the new **Swatches tab** or take advantage of colours in the **themed palettes** such as Earth, Pastel, and WebSafe. View currently open documents as thumbnails and load them via the **Documents tab** at the bottom of your workspace. Control text (e.g., captions) on the page with the **Character tab**—alter point size, letter spacing, width, and leading. Last but not least... the **How To tab** hosts topics describing commonly used operations, with access to supporting PhotoPlus Help and Tutorials.

- **Filter Gallery—filter enhancements** (p. 65)
  Zoom by **Alt**-dragging for greater visual control when previewing filters. Existing filters are enhanced—the **Add Noise** filter now supports Gaussian distribution, while results achieved with the **Emboss** filter will not disappoint! Not happy with a filter effect?—use the **Undo** button (unlimited undos) to revert back to previous effect settings.

Power

- **Versatile Layer management** (p. 103)
  Select adjacent or **non-adjacent multiple layers** for easy manipulation (group/ungroup, reorder, link/unlink, merging, arrange, make hidden, etc.). All unlinked or linked layers can be selected or deselected simultaneously. Align or distribute selected layers and any layers linked to the selected layers. Use the **Move Tool** to duplicate layers (by drag and drop) across documents—also use it to duplicate the selected layer within a document by **Alt**-dragging. Selection areas can also be dragged between documents.

- **Antialiased brush strokes** (p. 75)
  All brush strokes via the Paintbrush Tool now support **antialiasing**— achieve **smooth-edged** brush strokes every time compared to the new Pencil Tool's hard edging.

Ease of Use

- **In-Place text editing** (p. 98)
  For text placement, drag to size your text on-screen without restriction. Manipulate selected text **in situ** (no need to edit text via dialog)—apply different attributes to selected areas of text via the context toolbar and the new Character tab.

- **Independent layer movement for masking** (p. 117)
  For better photo positioning while masking, unlink a mask from its layer in the Layers tab—drag the independent layer within the mask shape (or just move the mask) to fine-tune the area visible.

- **Animation** (p. 128)
  For post-design tidy up, use **Flatten Frames** to make multi-layers into a single layer on a frame-by-frame basis. Fancy mirroring a frame's layer attributes such as position, visibility, effects, and many more, across selected or all frames?—try **Unify Layer Across Frames**. Instead of cloning a single frame, now **clone multiple frames** simultaneously.

- **.. and some enhancements you've been asking for!**
  Flip your drawn paths horizontally or vertically. The Layer tab's opacity slider previews while dragging. The **Flood Fill Tool** and **Colour Selection Tool** both now support antialiasing for smoother transitions. The **Colour** tab now hosts greyscale and foreground/background colour bar options. For **Layers, Channels** and **Paths** tabs, choose different thumbnail size options. **Scroll All Windows** or **Zoom All Windows** simultaneously when using the **Pan Tool** or **Zoom Tool** on multiple document windows. Show off your finished photo? Why not **Send** to your family, friends and colleagues as an email attachment?

Established Features

PhotoPlus brought professional image editing to everyone—with features like these:

- **EXIF and Raw Capture for digital camera users**
  View Exif information present on photos taken with a digital camera. Make changes to photos while still preserving Exif information by using **Save Original**. PhotoPlus directly opens the increasingly popular unprocessed RAW file formats from manufacturers such as Canon, Olympus and Nikon—over 150 digital camera models are supported!

- **Macros**
  Ever wanted to apply the same adjustment, effect or photo properties to multiple photos? The **Macros** feature enables you to automate your actions by using a huge number of categorized macro presets—alternatively, record and apply your own macro to any number of photos—give all your photos the same frame, age them or make a colour enhancement all at the same time!

- **Batch processing**
  Use batch processing to repeat your tasks, e.g. changing file types, all at the same time without user intervention. When used in conjunction with macros the possibilities are endless.

- **Editable QuickShapes**
  Easy to create, easy to change! Simply drag sliders to morph chevrons, hearts, badges, teardrops, moons, zigzags, and many more... apply layer effects and gradient fills... and edit any shape at any time. Create multiple shapes on a single layer—add, subtract, intersect, or exclude with previous shapes for frames, cutouts and custom contours. Draw directly as a Shape layer, path or as a filled bitmap on a raster layer.

- **Freehand and Bézier Curve and Shape Drawing**
  Powerful **vector-drawing tools** let you produce any shape under the sun with controllable, connectable, editable line segments.

- **Browse Image Files and Folders**
  The built-in Image Browser rapidly displays image thumbnails—a folder at a time—so you can preview clip art or saved work and inspect file details in a convenient, Explorer-style interface.

- **Unique Selection Options**
  PhotoPlus goes well beyond the basic rectangle and lasso tools, adding
  more than a dozen completely customizable selection shapes like
  polygons, spirals, and stars. Use Magnetic Selection to find edges as you
  trace them. Or define a selection shaped like text—using any font and
  style! Advanced options let you fine-tune the selection and its properties
  for smoother blends and precise effects. Paint to Select mode lets you
  literally "brush on" selectedness. Border, Threshold, and Smooth
  commands for more versatility. Store and load selections between any
  open file. Use combination buttons (as for shapes) to define cutout
  selection regions. Convert selections into paths or layers.

- **Paths**
  Use the full range of line- and shape-drawing tools to create editable
  outlines via the **Paths tab**. Convert paths to or from selections on any
  layer. "Stroke" paths using any brush to create bordered shapes!

- **Stamp and Spray**
  Use Picture Brushes to lay down colourful arrays of single or multiple
  mini-images: flowers, leaves, confetti, stars, and more...

- **Powerful Image Export Optimizer**
  The Export Optimizer lets you see how your image will look (and how
  much space it will take up) *before* you save it! Its multi-window display
  provides side-by-side WYSIWYG previews of image quality at various
  output settings, so you can make the best choice every time.

- **Web Animation Tools**
  It's easy and fun to create or edit animations for the Web. You can import
  and export animated GIFs, apply special effects (including 2D and 3D),
  tweening, even let PhotoPlus create entire animations for you
  automatically. Or export to the .AVI format for movies and multimedia!
  Convert to Animation makes the process of taking any image into
  animation mode a breeze!

- **Editable Text**
  Add formatted colour text to an image, reposition and scale it, integrate it
  with your design. Text layers keep the contents separate so you can go
  back and alter the words or formatting at any time!

- **Special Erase Options**
Need to remove that blue sky and leave the clouds? Use the Flood Eraser to fill the blue regions with transparency. Want to isolate a shape from a flat colour background? The Background Eraser samples pixels under the brush, so only unwanted colours drop out.

- **Filter Gallery**
The distort, blur, edge, render and other miscellaneous effects can be applied singularly or in combination within a **Filter Gallery**. The gallery possesses a large preview window in which to test the effect of your filters in turn...guaranteed to keep you up late!

- **Image Adjustments**
Apply professional, darkroom-style colour and histogram adjustments to your images—giving you fingertip control over tones and colours. Adjust **Shadow/Highlight/Midtone** to calm down overexposed skies in one single operation without having to resort to manipulating curves and levels. Employ the **Blur** and **Sharpen** tools to enhance or reduce local detail... blend multiple layers more cleanly. There's even a dedicated tool for removing "red eye" from flash photos.

- **Channels**
Use PhotoPlus's Channels tab to edit the Red, Green and Blue channels independently. This fine tuning enables noise to be reduced from the Green channel, blurring to be applied on the Blue channel and sharpening on the Red channel—all established methods for improving photo quality.

- **Histogram Support**
The Histogram is located in its own dockable tab and is "live". It dynamically responds to show the values for the currently active selection within your document. See how curves and level adjustments affect your image as they happen!

- **Editable Adjustment Layers**
Not only apply colour corrections and special effects, but store each change on a separate layer or group. To fine-tune any adjustment later, just click its layer and change the settings! The Instant Effects gallery puts 3D technology and layer effects at your disposal.

- **Special Effects**
A wild and whimsical assortment for instant creativity! Instant Artist effects turn your photos into **works of art**. PhotoPlus supports third-party Photoshop® plug-ins, and even lets you design your own custom filters.

- **2D Instant Effects**
  Add **Shadow, Glow, Bevel,** and **Emboss** layer effects for a sophisticated look on text or other image elements. Apply multiple effects onto a layer's existing effects for stunning design output. You can also copy and paste effects between layers.

- **Astounding 3D Lighting and Surface Effects**
  Advanced algorithms bring flat shapes to life! Vary surface and source **light properties.** Start with a pattern or a function, adjust parameters for incredible **surface contours, textures, fills.**

- **3D Painting using Depth Maps**
  Add **instant dimensionality** to your artwork. Painting or erasing on a layer's depth map appears as raised or lowered strokes on the image! Use with 3D layer effects to achieve "carved" side-view textures.

- **Versatile Deform and Warp Tools**
  The "Swiss Army Knife" of image tools, Deform lets you rotate, resize, skew, reshape, or add perspective to any selection or layer. Warp tools pull, stretch, and distort image details, or shrink and enlarge. Pixels turn to putty with the Mesh Warp tool! Use a customizable grid of points and lines to bend images with precision.

- **Gradient Fills**
  Take your pick of radial, linear, conical, or square fills—perfect for masking, to hide or reveal parts of your photo using smooth graduated blends to transparency. One **master dialog** allows editing of five gradient fill types combining both colour and transparency. Choose from a built-in gallery of presets, add your own categories and fills. (Of course, there's standard flood fill as well.)

- **Image Slicing and Image Maps**
  Now it's not just the pros who can use these techniques to add links to Web graphics! Simply click to divide images into segments—each with its own hyperlink and popup text—or add hotspots to specific regions. PhotoPlus outputs the HTML code and lets you preview the results directly in your Web browser.

- **Advanced Tools and Features**
  Built-in support for most pressure-sensitive graphics tablets. RGB, CMYK, HSL, and Greyscale colour modes. The Deform Mesh tool for reshaping any freeform region. Robust and convenient layer management with pop-up preview and masking support (on shape and text layers, too)! Extract command to isolate a face, feature, or object.

- **Professional Colour Management**
  ICC colour profiling means you'll achieve more accurate colours with specific monitors and printers—for printed output that more closely matches on-screen colours.

- **Professional Input and Output Options**
  Support for Photoshop® (.PSD) and Paint Shop Pro® (.PSP) files including translation of layers and effects where possible! And import Paint Shop Pro (.TUB) picture tubes to use as PhotoPlus Picture Brushes! Output using CMYK separations or print directly to your desktop printer with powerful controls (e.g., positional printing of single or multiple images). Portable Document Format (PDF) support for WYSIWYG electronic document delivery to web or pre-press. Include registration marks, crop marks, file information, greyscale and colour bars, and tile or scale your output if required.

- **Productive MDI Interface**
  A **Context toolbar** improves your efficiency by allowing the viewing and editing of a tool's properties in context with the tool currently selected. Open and view multiple images and edit them simultaneously. Dockable, resizeable floating **tab windows** work in conjunction with convenient toolbars and can be collapsed/expanded at any time—save your tab window positions, sizes, and docking settings to a workspace file (.wtb) for safe keeping. The **Navigator** and **Layers** tabs provide full control over all regions and planes. Each document stores a massive Undo range with dynamic memory and disk management, compressing information for optimized performance. Built-in **Autoselect** for rapid navigation in multi-layered images... handy **Measure Tool** for checking pixel dimensions... layout guides plus optional snapping to grid or guides for finer control when painting or erasing... the **History tab** so you never lose track of where you've been. And PhotoPlus remembers your preferred export settings, so your creative flow is undisturbed.

And that's only part of the story! The PhotoPlus feature set includes all the standard capabilities you'd expect in a photo editor. Tools like Paintbrush, Clone, Smudge, and Erase. Customizable brush tips, opacity, blend mode, and blend range settings. Flip, rotate, and crop. Antialiasing. TWAIN support for scanner and digital camera input. A full range of supported file formats for both import and export.

Registration, Upgrades, and Support

If you see the Registration Wizard when you launch PhotoPlus, please take a moment to complete the registration process. Follow the simple on-screen instructions and you'll be supplied a personalized registration number in return. If you need technical support please contact us, we aim to provide fast, friendly service and knowledgeable help. There's also a wide range of support information available 24 hours a day on our website at www.serif.com.

Installation

System requirements

If you need help installing Windows, or setting up your printer, see Windows documentation and help.

Minimum:

- Pentium PC with CD-ROM drive and mouse

- Microsoft Windows® 98 SE, Me, 2000, or XP operating system

- 128MB RAM (Windows 98 SE), see manufacturer's requirements for other operating systems

- 245MB (recommended install) free hard disk space

- SVGA display (800x600 resolution, 16-bit colour or higher)

Additional disk resources and memory are required when editing large and/or complex images.

Optional:

- Windows-compatible printer

- TWAIN-compatible scanner and/or digital camera

- Stylus or other input device, including pressure-sensitive pen

- Internet account and connection required for software auto-update

First-time install

To install PhotoPlus, simply insert the Program CD-ROM into your CD-ROM drive. The AutoRun feature automatically starts the Setup process and all you need to do is select the PhotoPlus Install option and answer the on-screen questions. If the AutoRun does not start the install, use the manual install instructions below.

Manual install/re-install

To re-install the software or to change any part of the installation at a later date, select **Settings/Control Panel** from the Windows **Start** menu and then click on the **Add/Remove Programs** icon. Make sure the correct CD-ROM is inserted into your CD-ROM drive, click the **Install...** button, and then simply follow the on-screen instructions. To install just one particular component to your hard drive, choose the Custom option and check only that component.

Getting Started

Seven Key Concepts

If you're new to photo editing programs, or perhaps have only worked with a basic painting program like Microsoft Paint, a number of the concepts in PhotoPlus may be new to you. Don't be daunted! Many thousands of artists have made the leap—the rewards are well worth it!

This section collects in one place some background material that should serve as a concise introduction and save you some "head-scratching" later on. We recommend you read through it before racing ahead to the rest of the chapter. And check out the "Key Concepts" tutorial for a hands-on walkthrough!

1 Image size and canvas size

Sometimes a tricky distinction if you haven't encountered it before, this is an important one when working with digital pictures. You probably know that image dimensions are given in **pixels** (think of pixels as the "dots of paint" that comprise a screen image)—say, 640 wide by 480 high. If you want to change these dimensions, there are two ways to go about it, and that's where **image** and **canvas** come into play. Changing the image size (I) means scaling the whole image or just a selected region up or down. Changing the canvas size (C), either by pixel or by relative percentage, means adding or taking away an area at the edges of the image—rather like adding a border around a mounted photo, or taking a pair of scissors and cropping the photo to a smaller size. Either way, after resizing, the image and canvas dimensions are once again identical.

2 Interacting tools and tabs

The **Tools toolbar** (see p. 24) is at the heart of PhotoPlus. Among its many offerings you'll find several basic **painting/drawing** tools, plus tools for **erasing**, **filling** a region, and **cloning** a region (all covered in detail in Chapter 4). As you try each of these tools, keep in mind that the **Context toolbar**, a properties bar that dynamically changes depending on which tool is selected, extends each tool's functionality by letting you customize its settings.

Tabs available in windows within the PhotoPlus workspace may also let you customize a tool's functionality, e.g. the **Brush Tip tab** can be used to set brush tip characteristics when using the Paintbrush Tool.

3 Making a selection

In any photo editing program, the **selection tools** (see Chapter 3) are as significant as any of the basic brush tools or commands. The basic principle is simple: quite often you'll want to perform an operation on just a portion of the image. The wide range of selection options in PhotoPlus lets you:

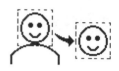

- Define just about any selection shape

- Modify the extent or properties of the selection

- Carry out various manipulations on the selected pixels, including cut, copy, paste, rotate, adjust colours, apply special effects, etc.

Although the techniques for using each selection tool vary a bit, the end result of making a selection is always the same: a portion of the image has been roped off from the rest of the image. The boundary is visible as a broken line or **marquee** around the selected region.

4 Foreground and background colours

At any given time, PhotoPlus allows you to work with just two colours—a **foreground** colour and a **background** colour. These are always visible as two overlapping swatches on the **Colour tab**. Electronic artists expend much of their creative energy deciding which of the millions of available colours should fill those two slots. The actual steps involved, however, can be quite simple (see p. 73).

5 Layers

If you're accustomed to thinking of pictures as flat illustrations in books, or photographic prints, the concept of **image layers** may take some getting used to. In

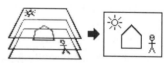

a typical PhotoPlus image—for example, a photograph you've scanned in, a new picture file you've just created, or a bitmap file you've opened—there is one layer that behaves like a conventional "flat" image. This is called the **Background layer**, and you can think of it as having paint overlaid on an opaque, solid colour surface. (Don't confuse the "background colour" with the "Background layer"—there's absolutely no connection!)

On top of the Background layer, you can create any number of new layers in your image. Each new one appears on top of another, comprising a stack of layers that you can view and manipulate with the Layers tab. We call these additional layers **standard layers** to differentiate them from the Background layer. Standard layers behave like transparent sheets through which the underlying layers are visible.

With few exceptions, you will work on just one layer at any given time, clicking in the Layers tab to select the current or **active layer**. Selections (see above) and layers are related concepts. Whenever there's a selection, certain tools and commands operate only on the pixels inside the selection—as opposed to a condition where nothing is selected, in which case those functions generally affect the entire active layer.

If your image has multiple layers, and you switch to another layer, the selection doesn't stay on the previous layer—it follows you to the new active layer. This makes sense when you realize that the selection doesn't actually include image content—it just describes a region with boundaries. And following the old advice "Don't confuse the map with the territory," you can think of the selection as a kind of outline map, and the active layer as the territory.

There are a few other special-purpose layers. For example, you can add **adjustment layers** (see p. 58) that let you try out effects on lower layers without actually applying them until you're ready to do so. PhotoPlus stores the text you create on **text layers**, while shapes go on **shape layers**. Both text and shape layers (see Chapter 5) work pretty much like standard transparent layers, and keep their respective elements editable so you can go back and make changes later.

We'll delve further into layers later in this chapter. Chapter 5 provides in-depth coverage.

6 Opacity and transparency

Opacity and **transparency** are complementary—like "half full" and "half empty." They both refer to the degree to which a particular pixel's colour contributes to the overall colour at that point in the image. (Pixels again are the "screen dots" that comprise a bitmap image in PhotoPlus.) Varying opacity is rather like lighting a gauze backdrop (scrim) in a theatre: depending on how light falls on it, it can be rendered either visible or invisible, or in between. Fully opaque pixels contribute their full colour value to the image. Fully transparent pixels are invisible: they contribute nothing to the image.

In-between pixels are called semi-transparent. You'll primarily encounter these terms in two contexts. First, as a property of the pixels laid down by individual **paint tools**, which can be more or less opaque, depending on the tool's opacity setting. Second, as a property of individual **layers**, where opacity works like a "master setting" that you can vary after paint has been laid down.

7 Saving and exporting

Saving a file in PhotoPlus means storing the image in the native PhotoPlus file format, using the **.SPP** extension. This format preserves image information, such as multiple layers, masks, or image map data, that would be lost in conversion to most other graphic formats. On the other hand, suppose you've opened a .BMP or .JPG file and want to save it back to its original format. In this case, you can use the **Save Original** command.

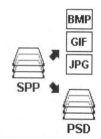

In yet another instance, you may be ready to save an .SPP file (or convert some other image type) to one of the standard graphics formats. In PhotoPlus, this is known as exporting. PhotoPlus includes a powerful **Export Optimizer** that serves as your "command centre" for exporting images to various formats. It not only provides a variety of options for each supported format, but lets you compare image quality using different settings and even retains your preferred settings for each format. And because PhotoPlus 11 is interoperable with Adobe Photoshop, if you export to Photoshop's .PSD format, image information (layers etc.) is preserved—just as if you'd saved to .SPP!

There's more on saving and exporting later in this chapter, and Chapter 8 includes details on file formats and optimizing images.

Starting PhotoPlus

Now that you've grasped the key concepts, let's start to explore PhotoPlus itself.

The Setup routine during install adds a **Serif PhotoPlus 11** item to the **Programs** submenu of the Windows **Start** menu.

- Use the Windows **Start** button to pop up the Start Menu and click on the PhotoPlus item.

PhotoPlus launches and displays the **Startup Wizard**, with a variety of choices:

- **open saved work** displays a browser that lets you preview and open saved image files—pictures in any supported format as well as animated GIFs.

- **create new picture** opens a new image window using a size and background colour you specify.

- **create new animation** opens a new image window and displays the Animation tab, with controls for creating animation frames.

- **view samples** opens the gallery of PhotoPlus images.

- **view tutorials** opens the easy-to-follow PhotoPlus Tutorials.

If you don't care to see the Startup Wizard again, uncheck the "use the startup wizard next time" box. However, we suggest you leave it checked until you're familiar with the equivalent PhotoPlus commands.

- Click **open saved work** and then click the **Browse** button in the dialog. PhotoPlus is set to initially display your PhotoPlus's Tutorials/Workspace folder (with some samples) but you can navigate to any folder from the dialog.

- Select an image and click **Open** to reveal the PhotoPlus user interface (in the following example, Wheel.jpg has been chosen). Your precise screen layout may vary somewhat from the illustration.

Getting Your Bearings

Now that you've got an image open, and the PhotoPlus menus and tools are available, let's take a quick look around the PhotoPlus environment. Even if you're in a rush to start working, don't skip the rest of the chapter! At the very least, take note of what's here so you'll know where to find the information when you need it later.

Introducing the interface

PhotoPlus can have multiple documents—images, in PhotoPlus terms—open at the same time. Each image window contains one image, with the image's name shown in the window's titlebar. At any given time, one image window will be **active** in front of any others, with its name shown in the main PhotoPlus titlebar.

You can use commands from the **Window** menu to arrange the image windows. If you have more than one image open, then you can switch to another window using the Window menu or the keyboard shortcut **Ctrl+Tab**. Double-click on an image window's titlebar to maximize it.

The PhotoPlus **toolbars** and **tab windows** (**tabs** for short) are essential features of the PhotoPlus environment. The *PhotoPlus Toolbars and Tabs* diagram on the next page identifies the principal toolbars and tabs and provides an overview of what they do.

A special type of toolbar is the **Context toolbar** whose tools and options dynamically change according to the type of tool selected in PhotoPlus. This ensures that the tool-specific options are always at your fingertips.

In the program, to display the related online help topic for any tab, first click the Help button on the top toolbar, then click the tab.

When you first launch PhotoPlus, it opens with the PhotoPlus toolbars and tabs all visible in default positions, with certain tabs "docked" or joined together. You can hide, show, or move them individually as needed, and dock or undock the tabs. Chances are you'll want to keep the Tools toolbar visible, but if your display area is large enough you might consider moving it to a horizontal position alongside the top (Standard) toolbar—or "floating" it as a separate palette. Remember, there's nothing fixed about the PhotoPlus interface, so feel free to try different arrangements until you're satisfied.

Principal PhotoPlus Toolbars and Tabs

Standard toolbar
Provides standard file and Clipboard commands, plus Zoom, Pan, Measure, and Web graphics tools.

Context toolbar
Access your tool properties quickly and easily with this dynamic toolbar

Photo Studio toolbar
Quickly access an impressive collection of correction/effect filters and artistic tools all hosted in studio environments

Tools toolbar
Features tools for selecting regions of the screen, painting and erasing, cropping and deforming selections, adding shapes and text, retouching... and more

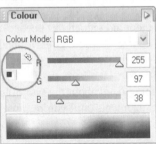

Colour tab
Lets you select foreground and background colours and change the colour mode

Brush Tip tab
Lets you choose and customize brush tips for the painting tools, define custom brushes

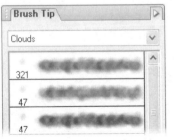

Instant Effects tab

Provides multiple categories of preset effects for spectacular textures and dimensionality

Histogram tab

Analyze your photo's distribution of colour pixels by specific or composite channel.

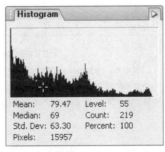

History tab

Maintains a record of PhotoPlus actions and lets you retrace your steps

Navigator tab

Lets you quickly see different parts of the image and change the zoom view

Layers tab
Controls for creating, deleting, arranging, merging, and setting properties of layers in the image

Paths tab
Stores independent outlines you can convert to (or from) selections, apply to any layer

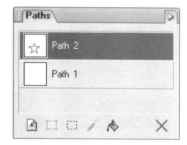

Macros tab
Lets you automate commands to increase your efficiency and productivity

Channels tab
View and set your composite and individual colour channels

Animation tab
Provides controls for editing animation files (only appears in Animation mode)

How To tab
Get quick answers to your "how to" questions by navigating around the Basics, Fixing Photos and Being Creative sections.

Swatches tab
Add colours you wish to use frequently to named categories. Select on-screen colour with the Colour Pickup Tool.

Character tab
Combines controls for dynamically fine-tuning text placement and properties.

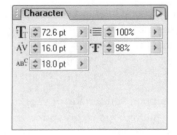

Documents tab

The tab displays your currently open document thumbnails at the bottom of your workspace. Use to navigate between open documents.

Here are some simple tab controls you might like to use:

- If you need more room on-screen for a particular operation, press the **Tab** key to turn all the visible tabs off, and again to turn them back on.

- To collapse a tab window, double-click the tab label of a selected tab (either separate or in a group). To expand, single-click the label.

- To turn a tab (or toolbar) off or on, uncheck or check its name on the View menu (tab names are listed under the **View Tabs** option.

- To reposition a tab, drag the tab by its tab label or gripper to its new position.

- To dock or undock a tab, double-click on its label or drag the tab label to the new position, either floating independently or docked in a window next to another tab.

Managing Workspace Tabs

At some point in your photo editing session you may want to save the layout of your tabs in the current workspace, with respect to positioning, their size, whether they are switched on/off and if docked or not. This is easy to achieve by selecting **Save Workspace tabs...** in the View menu. The settings are saved to a Workspace file (*.wtb) in a folder of your choice.

At any point you can **Reset Workspace Tabs...** to revert back to the default tab layout or **Load Workspace Tabs...** to load another previously saved Workspace .wtb file; both options are available via the View menu.

Note that your PhotoPlus tool properties and view settings remain unaffected.

Context toolbars

Context toolbars bring commonly used options to hand. If you're performing an operation on a layer, e.g. painting, applying text, drawing a line/shape, etc., it's really time-saving and less cumbersome to use the Context toolbar as a shortcut instead of navigating through menus or tabs. The Context toolbar does this well and, as its name suggests, the options shown will be specific to the currently selected tool. As an example, when the Paintbrush Tool is selected its brush options will be at hand on the Brush Context toolbar, i.e.

If you choose a different tool then the Context toolbar will change to the tool options associated with that newly selected tool.

As for other toolbars, the Context toolbar can be disabled if necessary from the View menu.

Setting preferences

To specify the ruler units, grid interval, and other preferences, choose **Preferences...** from the File menu to open the Preferences dialog. Select the appropriate options on the General, Undo, Transparency, Plugins, Layout, and/or Browser tab of the dialog. Note that switching off compression in Undo will provide faster performance.

Changes to the Plugins folder will not take effect until PhotoPlus is closed and restarted.

When you have made your choices, click the **OK** button to save your changes or click **Cancel** to abandon them.

Setting the view

Zooming (changing the relative size of the image in relation to its window) and **panning** (moving the image in relation to its window) are essential when you're operating at different levels of detail, or on different portions or an image. PhotoPlus provides standard Zoom and Pan tools, plus the **Navigator tab** which combines the best of both—it lets you quickly see different parts of the image and change the zoom view.

To change the image scale, choose the **Zoom Tool** on the Standard toolbar. To zoom in, left-click on the image. To zoom in on a particular region, drag with the tool to outline the region. To zoom out, right-click on the image. The current zoom percentage appears in the titlebar of the image window, next to the file name. By the way, if you have a wheel mouse, you can simply spin the wheel to change the zoom view!

You can also change the zoom ratio by choosing **Zoom In** or **Zoom Out** from the View menu. To restore a 1:1 viewing ratio, choose **Normal Viewing** from the View menu. To scale the window and image to the main PhotoPlus window, choose **Zoom to Fit**. To assist when performing detailed retouching, use **Zoom All Windows** on the Context toolbar to compare two pictures displayed side-by-side.

 To pan, choose the **Pan Tool** from the Standard toolbar (or press the spacebar) and drag the zoomed-in image to move it in relation to its window. A **Scroll All Windows** option on the Context toolbar lets you pan around side-by-side images at the same time.

The **Navigator tab** lets you quickly see different parts of the image and change the zoom view.

The red view box rectangle on the preview window marks the area of the image currently visible in the image window. You can drag it around or click the preview to change how the image is framed in its window.

Click the "-" magnifying glass icon to zoom out, "+" magnifying glass to zoom in, or drag the slider to change the zoom view. The current view ratio appears at the right.

How to Get an Image into PhotoPlus

Before you can manipulate an image, you'll need something to work with! PhotoPlus can open images saved in a wide variety of industry-standard file formats, acquire images from your TWAIN-compliant digital camera (or scanner) or perform screen capture.

To get a saved image into PhotoPlus, you select **Open Saved Work** from the Startup Wizard. The dialog displays image files you've recently worked on; select a file or click the **Browse** button to locate other saved files. As an alternative to using the Startup Wizard, you can select the name of a recently opened file from the File menu or choose **File>Open...** to display the Open dialog. The Open dialog shows dimensions and **bit depth** (see p. 149) information for each selected image.

Another option is to use the PhotoPlus Image Browser, which automatically creates thumbnails for images in the folders you open. To launch the Image Browser, choose **Image Browser...** from the File menu. Select source folders and preview thumbnails until you find the image you need. Right-click a thumbnail for information about the source image.

As a shortcut from either Windows Explorer or the Image Browser, you can simply drag and drop a file icon or preview thumbnail into PhotoPlus. You can even drag and drop an active selection from any OLE server application, such as another photo editor. If you drop onto an open PhotoPlus image window, the image data appears as a new layer. To open a new image window, drop onto a blank region within the main workspace.

If your scanner or digital camera supports the industry-wide **TWAIN** standard, you can bring pictures from these devices directly into PhotoPlus. (To set up your TWAIN device for importing, see the documentation supplied with the device for operating instructions.)

To begin scanning a picture into PhotoPlus, choose **Import** from the File menu and then select **Acquire**. If you have more than one TWAIN-compatible device installed, you may be prompted to select one as the source—or you can specify a different source by choosing **Import>Select Source...** from the File menu.

The acquisition software for the selected device will start up and display its window, and you can then carry out the scan, possibly having made a few basic adjustments. Note that the features available in image acquisition software vary widely and are not under the control of PhotoPlus. Usually, you will at least be able to adjust settings for the image source (such as a colour photograph, black and white photograph, or colour halftone) and the resolution at which the image is to be scanned. For colour theory and tips on scanning, see p. 158.

Whether you import the image via the Open dialog or the TWAIN interface, it will appear in a new image window in PhotoPlus. Assuming the image is not in the native PhotoPlus (.SPP) format or the Adobe Photoshop (.PSD) format, it will always have just a single layer, called the **Background layer**. Chapter 5 will explore layers in considerable detail; until then we'll be focusing on techniques that work perfectly well on one—or at most two—layers.

Once you've opened an image, you can create an instant working copy in a new window by choosing **Duplicate...** from the Image menu. To revert to the saved version of the current image, choose **Revert** from the File menu.

Whichever method you've chosen to add photo(s) to PhotoPlus you may have noticed a **Documents tab** at the bottom of your PhotoPlus workspace. This tab handily displays all of your currently open documents, in either saved (shows file name) or unsaved state (shows, e.g. "Untitled1"). Click on any document thumbnail to maximize and promote your document in the front of other open documents. You can also right-click to Minimize, Maximize, Restore, or Close any document.

Screen Capture

Another method of getting images into PhotoPlus is **Screen Capture**, which offers a choice of elements which you can choose to capture. An Active Window, the Client Area (the entire PhotoPlus program environment), Full Screen or Selected Object (or Area) can all be set to be captured via **Screen Capture>Options...** on the File menu. To add a capture delay, check the **Delay** box and specify a time (in seconds) which allows you to setup your screen display (e.g., menu flyouts). Optionally, you can also include your cursor in your screen capture—great for pointing out how to perform a selection!

For example, if you wanted to show off PhotoPlus's Colour tab (and colour selection) you can capture it with ease—note the inclusion of the cursor.

How do you actually initiate a capture? You can enter capture mode by selecting either:

- **Capture Now** button from Screen Capture>Options....
  OR

- **Screen Capture>Start** on the File menu.

All that's now required is to press the hot key (normally **F11** key but configurable in **Screen Capture>Options...** to be any key from F1 to F11). For Selected Area Capture you have to position the crosshair guides, and drag to enclose the selected area (use the supporting magnification tool's guides to fine-tune your selected area).

Whatever you choose to capture, the resulting captured image will be displayed in an untitled window. You can copy and paste as a new image/layer in an existing project or save in a new project. Alternatively, you can export as an image directly via the Export Optimizer.

To capture again, you must re-enter capture mode.

If you have a multi-monitor display, Screen Capture can only capture on your primary monitor and will not work on any of your secondary monitors.

Saving and Exporting Files

PhotoPlus can save images in its own .SPP format, or export them to any standard format (see Seven Key Concepts on p. 17).

Use **File>Save** (or click the **Save** button) to save images in PhotoPlus's own .SPP format. SPP images preserve information such as multiple layers, masks, or image map data that would be lost in conversion to almost any other graphic format (the one exception is the Photoshop .PSD format).

Use **File>Save As...** to save the image as an .SPP file under a different path or name.

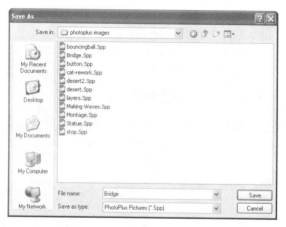

You can store files anywhere on your system. It's a good idea to group your images, for example into project-oriented or thematic folders.

Suppose you've opened a .BMP or .JPG file, done some editing (without adding layers), and now wish to save it back to its original format. In this case, you can use the **File>Save Original** or **File>Save Original As...** command. Using the former will overwrite the original file—so be sure that's what you want to do.

In many situations, you'll want to save a file to one of the standard graphics formats. In PhotoPlus, this is known as **exporting**. You can use the **Export Optimizer** to preview image quality before at various settings before going ahead with the export.

The File menu offers two ways of accessing the Optimizer. Either choose **File>Export Optimizer...** to display it directly, or choose **File>Export...** and then click the **Optimizer** button in the dialog. The Export dialog itself is a standard file dialog where you can specify the path, name, and format for the image file.

The Export Optimizer consists of a left-hand preview display and a right-hand settings region, with additional buttons along the left of the dialog. In animation mode, there's an extra tab for changing output settings.

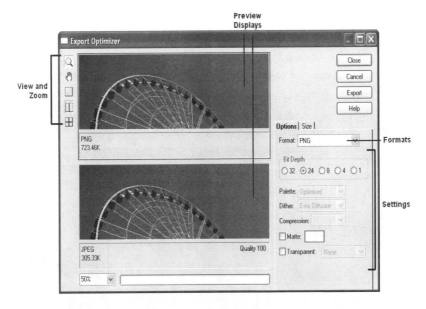

To display a different portion of the image, drag the image in the preview pane. To change the display scale, choose the **Zoom** button at the left, then left-click to zoom in or right-click to zoom out (or choose a zoom percentage at the lower left).

To adjust the preview display, click one of the **View** buttons at the left to select Single, Double, or Quad display. The illustration above shows Double view. The multi-pane (Double and Quad) settings let you compare different export settings for one or more file formats. Just click one of the display panes to select it as the active pane, then use the Options panel at the right to choose an export format and specific settings. Each time you make a new choice, the active pane updates to show the effect of filtering using the new settings, as well as the estimated file size!

The Options tab lets you pick a preferred export format, tailor the settings—including transparency and matte (background) colour—to your needs. Use the Size tab if you need to scale the image (typically downward, to preserve quality) or squash it horizontally or vertically. When you've picked the optimum export settings, click the dialog's **Export** or **OK** button to proceed to the Export dialog. Again, since the exported image is stored separately from your original .SPP file, you won't have altered the master file at all.

For details on image file formats and optimization, see p. 125.

Print Output

PhotoPlus provides several print-based output options: standard **single-image** printing, **multi-image** printing, and **PDF** (Portable Document Format) export. We'll cover standard printing here; see Chapter 8 for coverage of multi-image and PDF output.

To print a single image, choose **Print...** from the File menu, click the **Print** button on the Standard toolbar, or press **Ctrl+P**.

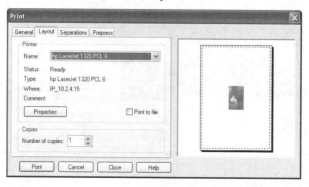

The General tab provides basic control over printed output, and the preview on the right shows the margins of the printable page. Choose a printer from the drop-down list; if necessary, click the **Properties** button to set up the printer for the correct page size, etc. It's very important to set up your printer correctly to get the best results. Select the Layout, Separations, and/or Prepress tabs if you need to set special options such as scaling, tiling, CMYK colour separations, or printer marks. (These advanced print options are detailed in Chapter 8.)

After setting the printer properties and the print options, click the **Print** button to send the image to the printer. Depending on the size and complexity of the image, and the printer you're using, it may take several minutes before the printed page emerges.

You can also use the **Print Multiple** command (see p. 164) to position one or more images precisely on the printed page.

Sharing documents by email

The widespread availability of the Internet means that colleagues, family and friends are now only a quick email away. Higher line speeds via Broadband connections open up new opportunities for sharing documents in their native file format (.SPP) or as converted JPGs.

PhotoPlus lets you send your currently selected document to your standard email program (e.g., Outlook) for subsequent mailing. You can do this by choosing **Send...** from the File menu to display a dialog which sets the file type and image size restrictions.

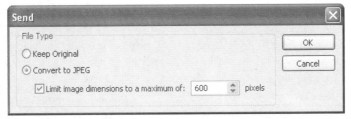

After this, if the email program is not loaded, a Choose Profile dialog lets you select your email program, then a new email message is displayed with document attached. If already loaded, your email program automatically attaches your document to a new email message.

To complete the process, press the Send button (or equivalent) on your email program as for any other email message.

Setting the file type

To take advantage of better file compression you may want to convert your image to JPEG if not already in this format. The conversion would be suitable if your original document was in TIF format or was a very complex multi-layered SPP file.

From the above dialog, send the original SPP file by enabling the **Keep Original** radio button. To convert to JPEG and send as such, click the **Convert to JPEG** radio button.

Setting your image size

PhotoPlus allows you to send any photo directly by email with an added file size limiter if necessary. This avoids sending excessively large files—this could affect your popularity!

Click the **Limit image dimensions to a maximum of** check box and select a suitable image resolution—this will be the new pixel height or width (the biggest pixel dimension of the original photo will be reduced to the new image size). Alternatively, keep original image dimensions by leaving the option unchecked.

An Internet connection is required for the emailing of pictures.

Manipulating Images

This chapter will focus firstly on ways of manipulating existing photos, and secondly on applying correction and special effect filters to enhance visual appeal. Note that all of the techniques described here can also be applied to images created from scratch.

There are many reasons why you might want to manipulate a photo, including:

- Cleaning up an old, damaged photo

- Removing an unwanted item or slogan from the background

- Preparing an image for printing, use on the web, or in another package

By the way, if you make a mistake, don't worry. Most actions in PhotoPlus can be undone using **Undo** from the Edit menu, the **Undo** button on the Standard toolbar, or the keyboard shortcut **Ctrl+Z**. You can even undo an "undo"—use **Redo** on the Edit menu, the Standard toolbar, or with **Ctrl+Y**. (The **File>Preferences...** dialog lets you set options for the Undo function.) Or you can use the History tab to review recent actions and jump back more than one step at a time.

Making Selections

Before you can apply work on specific areas of your picture, or copy parts of a picture to the Clipboard, you must define an active selection area.

Selection options

Many times you'll want to select just a subset of the image (or layer) to work on. Selecting, you may recall, was one of the "Key Concepts" (see p. 17). Understanding what you can do with selections opens up exciting creative possibilities.

Whenever there's a selection, certain tools and commands operate only on the pixels inside the selection—as opposed to a condition where nothing is selected, in which case those functions generally affect the entire active layer. For example, when there's a selection, the brush tools only work inside the selection; the colour simply doesn't affect outside pixels. If you apply an adjustment or special effect from the Image or Effects menus, it only affects the selected region.

Clicking a layer's name on the Layers tab makes it the active layer. To select the whole active layer, choose **Select All** from the Select menu or press **Ctrl+A**. To select just opaque pixels, **Ctrl**-click the layer thumbnail. To deselect use **Ctrl+D**.

PhotoPlus offers a very wide range of selection methods, and a variety of commands for modifying the extent or properties of the selected pixels.

The standard selection tools are located on the **Standard Selection Tools** flyout on the Tools toolbar. There you can choose from the Rectangle, Ellipse, Freehand, Polygon, or Magnetic selection tools.

To select a rectangular or elliptical area, select the **Rectangle** or **Ellipse Selection** tool from the flyout and drag to define a region on the image.

Rectangle / Square   **Ellipse / Circle**

The selected region is bounded by a broken line or **marquee**, and the cursor over the selection changes to the Move Marquee cursor, which lets you reposition just the marquee as needed without affecting the underlying pixels.

Holding down the **Ctrl** key during dragging constrains the selection shape to either a square or a circle. If the Snapping feature is enabled (via **View>Snapping** or the button on the HintLine), the marquee's edges jump as you drag to align with visible grid points, guide lines, and/or document edges. (See "Using screen layout tools" in PhotoPlus help for details.)

To select a freehand (irregular) area, select the **Freehand Selection Tool** and just drag to draw around the area to be selected, making a closed area.

Or use the **Polygon Selection Tool** to draw a series of line segments (double-click to close the polygon).

Freehand   **Polygon**

The **Adjustable Selection Tools** flyout, a unique PhotoPlus feature, offers 20 different variable selection shapes, including star, arrow, heart, spiral, wave, and so on.

Here's how the adjustable selection tools work. We'll use the regular polygon selection shape as an example. Choose a tool from the flyout and drag out a shape on the image. You can hold down the **Ctrl** key to constrain the shape (to a circle or square).

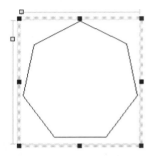

The regular polygon appears as an outline with two slider tracks bounding it. Each of the slider tracks has a square handle, and when you move the cursor on to the handle it will change to a + sign. As you drag the sliders, the shape's properties change. In the case of the polygon, one slider varies the number of sides, while the other rotates the shape. Once you're satisfied with the selection, double-click in the centre (just as with the Crop Tool or Magnetic selection tool) to complete the marquee. The shape will then possess a dashed outline.

The 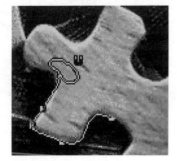 **Magnetic Selection Tool** makes it easy to isolate part of an image where there's already a bit of an edge showing. You simply trace around the edge, and PhotoPlus snaps the selection marquee to the nearest dramatic colour change. Click once on the image to place a starting node along an edge. With the mouse button up, trace along the edge; the marquee line follows the nearest edge. At regular distances, nodes automatically appear along the line. Only the portion of the line beyond the last node remains adjustable.

You can add a node manually (for example, at a corner), by clicking once, or "back up" by pressing **Delete** to undo recent nodes one at a time. To close the selection region, double-click or click again on the starting node. On the Context toolbar, you can adjust the tool's **Frequency** (distance between automatic nodes) and **Contrast** (edge sensitivity) for best results. As a shortcut, press the up and down arrow keys (or use your mouse's spinwheel) to adjust the contrast setting on the fly.

If you're trying to lift a region away from its background and find the Magnetic Selection Tool still too laborious, try the Edit menu's **Extract...** command (also on the Photo Studio toolbar). This lets you mark the edge contour rapidly using a broad brush, and then apply edge-detection within the swath you've marked. Note that Extract directly affects the layer or selection—pixels outside the detected edge vanish to transparency, while interior pixels are preserved. (See online help for details.)

Using the **Colour Selection Tool**, you can select a region based on the colour similarity of adjacent pixels—choose the tool from the Tools toolbar and then click on a starting pixel. This selects the pixel you clicked, and any adjacent pixels that are similar in colour, as measured by the **Tolerance** value shown on the Context toolbar (see p. 80). You can raise or lower the tolerance setting to include more or fewer pixels. You may want to select colour on all layers with the **Use all layers** option (rather than the current layer), or **Antialias** edges for smoother selection—both available on the Context toolbar.

As a more intelligent colour selection method, i.e. where selection is based on "tagging" a specific range of colours in the image, choose **Colour Range...** from the Select menu. To initially tag a particular colour group, such as "Reds" or "Midtones", choose the group's name from the **Select** drop-down list. Alternatively, you can tag a range by hand: click the **Colour Picker** button and click over a chosen colour in the Preview window (with this method, the Tolerance slider lets you include a wider or narrower range of colours in the selection).

Once you've made an initial selection, you can use the **Add Colour** and **Subtract Colour** buttons and drag to tweak the tagged range. Meanwhile, the dialog provides visual feedback. If **Show Selection** is checked, the greyscale Selection window on the right shows tagged values as brighter, with untagged pixels darker. You can customize what's displayed in the Preview window on the left by picking an option from the Preview list: "None" shows the original image, "White Matte" shows tagged pixels through a white background, and so on.

PhotoPlus also offers a **Text Selection Tool** that lets you create a text-shaped selection region and vary its size or font (see the next chapter).

Modifying the selection

Once you've used a selection tool to select a region, you can carry out a number of additional steps to fine-tune the selection before you actually apply an effect or manipulation to the selected pixels.

Any time you're using one of the selection tools, the cursor over a selected region changes to the Move Marquee cursor, which lets you drag the marquee outline to reposition it. You can also use the keyboard arrows to "nudge" the selection. In this case you're *only* moving the selection outline—not the image content inside it. You use the Move Tool (see p. 48) to drag the selection *plus* its image content.

If the selection you've made isn't quite the right shape, or doesn't quite include all the necessary pixels (or perhaps includes a few too many), you can continue to use the selection tools to add to, or subtract from, the selected region. To add to the existing selection, drag with the selection tool while holding down the **Shift** key. To subtract, drag while holding down the **Alt** key. Pressing the **Ctrl** key changes the tool temporarily to the Move Tool, so you can move the selection's content.

When a standard selection tool is active, the Context toolbar includes combination buttons (**New**, **Add**, **Subtract**, and **Intersect**) that determine the effect of each new operation with a selection tool. Starting with a standard square selection, here's what a second selection operation might produce with the other combination settings:

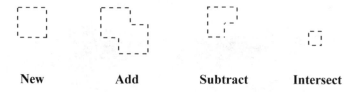

| New | Add | Subtract | Intersect |

For Rectangle and Ellipse Selection tools, the Context toolbar additionally lets you set a **Fixed Size** or **Fixed Aspect**, or number of **Rows** or **Columns** (Rectangle Selection Tool only) in advance of creating your selection—great if you have a clear idea of the selection area required!

Alternatively, the **Modify** item on the Select menu provides a submenu with several functions that gives you the option of hand-drawing to change the selection boundaries. Choose **Contract...** to shrink the borders of the selection, or **Expand...** to extend its borders. **Border...** creates a new selection as a "frame" of a specified pixel width around the current selection. If the selected area has ragged edges or discontinuous regions (for example, if you've just used the Colour Selection tool), you can use the **Smooth...** command to even them out.

Grow and **Similar** both expand the selection by seeking out pixels close (in colour terms) to those in the current selection. **Grow** only adds pixels adjacent to the current selection, while **Similar** extends the selection to any similar pixels in the active layer. Both use the current tolerance value entered for the Colour Selection Tool (see p. 44).

To remove the current selection, choose **Deselect** from the Select menu, or use the keyboard shortcut **Ctrl+D**.

The **Invert** command on the Select menu selects the portion of the active layer outside the current selection. Unselected pixels become selected, and vice versa.

Variable selections

Just as greyscale is more than black-and-white, a selection can be more complex than an all-or-nothing proposition. Within the selected/marqueed region, individual pixels can have varying degrees of "selectedness."

Antialiasing and **feathering** are properties of the various selection tools that can help you achieve softer edges and smoother blending of elements that are being combined in the image. You can control either option for the Standard and Adjustable Selection tools, using the **Feather** input box (or slider) and **Antialias** check box on the Context toolbar. Antialiasing makes the selection's edge pixels semi-transparent, while feathering reduces the sharpness of a selection's edges not by varying transparency, but by *partially selecting* edge pixels. If you lay down paint on a feathered selection, the paint will actually be less intense around the edges.

You can apply feathering "after the fact" to an existing selection (but before applying any editing changes) using the Select menu's **Modify>Feather...** command. **Modify>Threshold** converts a feathered, soft-edged selection into a hard-edged selection. As with feathering, you won't see an immediate effect on the image, but painting and other editing operations will work differently inside the selection.

Paint to Select mode is a convenient way to achieve varying degrees of selectedness on a layer. Using the standard painting and editing tools in this mode, you can create a selection from scratch or modify an existing selection. Check **Paint to Select** on the Select menu and the image view switches to indicate selected regions using a coloured mask. Choose **Select>Paint to Select Options** to specify whether to mask selected or unselected areas, and which colour and opacity to use. In the default view, fully selected regions are masked 50% with red and semi-selected regions appear pinkish, while deselected regions have no colouration. In Paint to Select mode you can paint or use other manipulations on the temporary mask to directly modify the selection according to the lightness of the colours you apply. Painting in white adds to the selection; black subtracts from it; grey creates partial selection.

This view shows "selectedness" much more clearly than the standard marquee mode, so it's also a good way to preview or check a complex selection.

In the illustration below, (A) depicts the incomplete result of using the Magnetic Selection tool on a white flower. In Paint to Select mode (B) the selected regions appear as red (grey here) and we are busy filling in the selected regions with a white brush. (C) shows the completely filled-in flower and (D) the fully selected result.

| A | B | C | D |

Color Selection   Painting (in white) -   Resulting
tool result   in Paint to Select mode   selection

Once you have selected precisely the pixels you want to work on (as covered
so far in this chapter), the question arises: what can you *do* with the
selection—or technically speaking, with the pixels you've outlined? The rest
of the chapter will survey the many possible manipulations you can perform.

Using the Move Tool

The **Move Tool** (unlike the Move Marquee cursor associated with the
selection tools) is for pushing actual pixels around. With it, you can drag the
contents of a selection from one place to another, rather than just moving the
selection outline. To use the tool, simply click on the selection and drag to the
new location (or use the keyboard arrows to nudge). The selected part of the
image moves also. If the Snapping feature is enabled (via **View>Snapping** or
the HintLine button), the moved region's edges align with visible grid points,
guide lines, and/or document edges.

If nothing is selected, dragging with the Move Tool moves the entire active
layer. (Or, if the Move Tool's **Automatically select layer** property is selected
on the Context toolbar, the tool intelligently moves to the first visible layer.)
Moving image content on the Background layer exposes a "hole" that appears
in the current background colour; on standard layers, the exposed region is
transparent.

To duplicate the contents of the selection on the active layer, press the **Alt** key
and click, then drag with the Move Tool.

As a shortcut if you're working with any one of the selection tools, you can
press the **Ctrl** key to switch temporarily to the Move Tool. Press **Ctrl+Alt** to
duplicate. Release the key(s) to revert to the selection tool.

Cut, Copy, Paste, Delete

These operations work pretty much as you'd expect. You can use the buttons on the Standard toolbar, choose commands from the Edit menu, or use conventional keyboard shortcuts.

As with the Move Tool, "holes" appear as either the current background colour or transparent, depending which layer you're working on.

When pasting from the Clipboard, PhotoPlus offers several options. The standard paste (**Ctrl+V**) operation creates a new, untitled image window. You can use other Edit menu choices to paste the Clipboard contents as a new layer (**Ctrl+L**), or centred into the current selection (**Shift+Ctrl+L**). The **Into Selection** option is useful if you're pasting from one layer to another. Because the selection marquee "follows" you to the new layer, you can use it to keep the pasted contents in registration with the previous layer.

Cropping

Cropping is the electronic equivalent of taking a pair of scissors to a photograph, except of course with a pair of scissors there is no second chance! Cropping deletes all of the pixels outside the crop selection area, and then resizes the image canvas so that only the area inside the crop selection remains.

Select the **Crop Tool** from the Tools toolbar and drag out a rectangular unconstrained crop selection area on the image. (Hold down the **Ctrl** key while dragging to constrain the selection to a square.) Adjust the selection rectangle as needed, then double-click within the crop area (or select the tick button on the Context toolbar) to complete cropping.

It's also possible to crop to a pre-defined portrait or landscape print size (e.g., 4 x 6 in or 6 x 4 in, respectively), so that the print resolution adjusts automatically to honour the print dimensions. To do this, choose the **Crop Tool** and select the print size from the first drop-down menu on the displayed Context toolbar. Custom print sizes can instead be specified in the subsequent width and height drop-down menus.

The Context toolbar also hosts a **Thirds** grid which helps photo composition when cropping—position a focal point of interest on any one of the four intersection points on the grid for best results.

You can crop an image to any selection region, no matter what shape, as defined with one of the selection tools.

- Make a selection using one of the selection tools and then choose **Crop to Selection** from the Image menu. For example, here's cropping applied to a marquee drawn with the Freehand Selection Tool:

If the selection region is non-rectangular, the left-over surrounding region will be either transparent (on a standard layer) or the background colour (on the Background layer).

Tip: To convert the Background layer to a standard layer, right-click **Background** on the Layers tab and choose **Promote to Layer**. Now operations on the layer's content (such as moving, cutting, or irregular cropping) will leave transparent "holes."

Flipping, Rotating, and Deforming

Flipping and rotating are standard manipulations that you can carry out on the whole image, the active layer, path, or just on a selection.

To flip, choose either **Flip Horizontally** or **Flip Vertically** from the Image menu, then select **Image**, **Layer**, **Selection** or **Path** from the submenu. If you flip an image horizontally, be careful not to accidentally reverse things like text, numbers, and so on.

To rotate, choose **Rotate...** from the Image menu and select an option: the object (Image, Layer, or Selection), rotation angle (90°, 180°, or enter a custom angle), and the direction (clockwise or anticlockwise). The image will rotate about the centre point.

Original image   *15° anti-clockwise*   *10° clockwise*

 For image correction, the **Straighten Tool** can be used to align a crooked image back to vertical. Use the tool to trace a new horizon line against a line in the image (simply drag and release the horizon line)—the image automatically orients itself to the drawn horizon line. The supporting Context toolbar lets you choose how your straightened image is displayed; select from **Crop** (to remove border), **Expand to Fit** or **Original Size**. Subsequent cropping of the image is needed to redefine your vertical and horizontal image edges.

The **Deform Tool** is a "Jack of all trades" that lets you move, scale, rotate, or skew a selection or layer. Try it on a text layer for unique results! Start by making a selection if desired, then choose the tool. A rectangle appears with handles at its corners and edges, and a fixed point (initially in the centre of the region). If there's no selection, the rectangle includes the whole active layer.

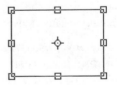

The tool's action depends on the exact position of the mouse pointer. As you move the pointer around the enclosed region, the cursor changes as shown below to indicate which action is possible.

►   To **move the region** without any deformation, drag from its neutral midsection. This action works just like the Move Tool.

     To **reshape the region**, drag from an edge or corner handle. A variety of options are available when you drag from a corner (watch the HintLine for tips). You can resize vertically and/or horizontally, either with or without a constant aspect ratio (use the **Shift** key for a fixed aspect ratio). In addition, you can get skew or perspective effects that move either one corner by itself, or two adjacent corners! Hold down the **Ctrl** key while dragging to skew the object. For perspective effects, press **Shift+Ctrl+Alt** while dragging from an object's corner.

 To **rotate the region** about the fixed point, drag from just outside a corner. To constrain rotation in 15-degree steps, press the **Shift** key after you've begun rotation, and hold it down until after you release the mouse button.

 To **reposition the fixed point**, move the cursor to the exact centre until a small target appears, then drag. The fixed point can be moved anywhere—even outside the deformation region.

The **Selection Deform Tool** on the Tools toolbar's Deform Tools flyout lets you transform, scale or rotate any already drawn selection area. With the tool enabled, square nodes on the midpoints and corners of any selected area can be dragged—look for the cursor changing between resize and rotate modes when hovering over a corner node. Use in conjunction with the **Ctrl** key to transform the area independently, creating a skewed transform. The **Alt** key resizes the area about its centre, while the **Shift** key maintains the area's aspect ratio. It's also possible to move the small centre of rotation "handle" in the centre of the transform to produce an arc rotational movement rather than rotating around the area's centre. You can hold down the **Shift** key whilst rotating to cause movement in 15° intervals.

Note that you can still apply layer effects, fills, and other manipulations to deformed image content. And once you have rotated or deformed text, you can still edit it as long as it's on a text layer!

Using Mesh Warp

The **Mesh Warp Tool** works like the Deform Tool outfitted with complex curves. It lets you define a flexible grid of points and lines that you can drag to distort an image, or part of an image (or layer). You can edit the mesh to vary its curvature, and even custom-design a mesh to match a particular image's geometry, for more precise control of the warp effect.

When you first select the tool, a simple rectangular mesh appears over the image, with nine nodes: one at each corner, one at the centre, and one at the midpoint of each edge. Straight lines connect adjacent nodes. The Context toolbar also changes to reflect the settings appropriate to the Mesh Warp Tool.

These "straight" line segments are actually bendable curves. When you alter the contours of the mesh and distort the initial rectangular grid, the underlying image deforms accordingly. To change the mesh, you simply move nodes, handles, or connecting lines; add or subtract nodes as needed; and/or edit nodes to change the curvature of adjoining lines.

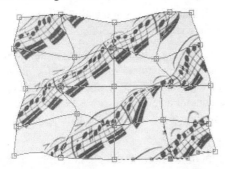

To **select a mesh node**, click it. (**Shift**-click or drag a marquee to select multiple nodes.) One or more **attractor handles** appear on the selected node(s) and on any adjacent nodes.

To **warp the mesh**, drag any mesh node or line segment, or drag a node's attractor handles. The image responds immediately as the mesh is warped.

 To **add a new node**, double-click on a line segment or click the **Add Node** button on the Context toolbar.

 To **delete** nodes, select them and press **Delete**, or click the **Delete Node** button on the Context toolbar.

 The **Deform Mesh Tool** on the Context toolbar makes it easy to move, scale, skew, or rotate a portion of the mesh about a fixed point. It works just like the standard Deform tool (described above) on multiple nodes.

The bendability of line segments depends on the type of nodes at either end. You can change a node from one type to another simply by selecting it and using the Context toolbar buttons:

 Sharp Corner means that the curves on either side of the node are completely independent, so the contours can be adjusted separately.

 Smooth Corner means that the slope of the curve is the same on both sides of the node, but the depth of the contours on either side can differ.

 Symmetric Corner nodes join curves with the same slope and depth on both sides of the node.

See PhotoPlus online help for further details on Mesh Warp.

Channels

Before looking into adjusting colour in images and applying special effects, it's a good time to look at colour channels in PhotoPlus.

It goes without saying that every colour photo that you use in PhotoPlus will have channels associated with it. For the colour mode RGB, the individual channels will be Red (R), Green (G) and Blue (B), plus a combined channel called the composite RGB channel. Each channel stores that particular colour's information, which when combined with the other channels, bring about the full colour image.

Within PhotoPlus, the use of multiple layers could possibly confuse the user with respect to understanding channels. What do the channels refer to? —the entire photo, part of it, a layer? The answer is simple—channels are always a colour sub-set of the active selected layer, whether this is a background, standard, shape or text layer. Remember that an imported photo will have a single background layer by default.

PhotoPlus lets you show, hide, and select channels of any photo from a single point, called the **Channels** tab. This tab lists the composite RGB and each individual Red, Green and Blue channel in turn.

Channels can be shown or hidden by clicking the eye icon next to the channel. When the eye is open the channel is visible. The composite RGB channel is shown only when all the other channels are shown. When a single or pair of single channels is shown the composite channel will never be shown. Give it a try—remember to study the effect this has on your photo.

An equally powerful feature of the Channels tab is the opportunity to select individual channels for edit. By default, all channels are selected and visible (as shown previously). However, you can select an individual channel by simply clicking the RGB, Red, Green or Blue entry once—then apply a change to it in isolation. Note that this also hides all other channels at the same time. The selected channel(s) can be viewed as greyscale or in colour by checking the **Show Channels in Colour** option (click the button on the tab).

Why do we want to select channels anyway? This is because you can apply an edit to a selected individual channel in isolation. Typically, you could:

- Apply a filter effect

- Make an image adjustment

- Paint onto a channel

- Use the magic wand

- Paste selections

- Fill the channel

- ... and many more!

This is because a colour channel is treated as a subset of a layer, so anything you could apply to a layer can pretty much be applied to a channel.

Adjusting Image Values

PhotoPlus provides a number of different adjustment filters that you can apply to a selection or to a standard layer. Typically, these adjustments are used to correct deficiencies in the original image. You can apply them either directly, via the **Image>Adjust** menu, or (in most cases) by using an **adjustment layer**.

Each of the adjustment options works in a similar way. Alter the values by dragging on a slider, moving it to the left to decrease the value, or the right to increase the value, or enter a value in the field at the right of the slider.

Tip: Instead of dragging the slider with the mouse, you can click on it and then jog it with the left or right cursor arrow keys.

Here's a quick summary of the PhotoPlus image adjustments (see PhotoPlus help for an in-depth description).

- **AutoLevels** and **AutoContrast** redistribute the lightness (luminance) values in the image, making the darkest image pixel black and the lightest one white, and adjusting the spread in between. AutoLevels performs this adjustment separately for each of the Red, Green, and Blue channels, while AutoContrast operates on the image as a whole.

- **Levels** pops up a dialog that affords more precise control than either AutoLevels or AutoContrast. While viewing a histogram plot of lightness values in the image, you can adjust the tonal range by shifting dark, light, and gamma values.

- **Curves** displays lightness values in the image using a line graph, and lets you adjust points along the curve to fine-tune the tonal range.

- **Colour Balance** lets you adjust colour and tonal balance for general colour correction in the image.

- **Brightness/Contrast: Brightness** refers to overall lightness or darkness, while **contrast** describes the tonal range, or spread between lightest and darkest values. (See example on p. 59.)

- **Shadow/Highlight/Midtone** controls the extent of shadows, highlights, and contrast within the image.

- **Hue/Saturation/Lightness: Hue** refers to the colour's tint—what most of us think of as rainbow or spectrum colours with name associations, like "blue" or "magenta." **Saturation** describes the colour's purity—a totally unsaturated image has only greys. **Lightness** is what we intuitively understand as relative darkness or lightness—ranging from full black at one end to full white at the other.

- **Replace Colour** lets you "tag" one or more ranges of the full colour spectrum that require adjustment in the image, then apply variations in hue, saturation, and/or brightness to just those colour regions (not to be confused with the simpler Replace Colour Tool; see p. 61).

- **Selective Colour** lets you add or subtract a certain percentage of cyan, magenta, yellow, and/or black ink for creating effects.

- **Channel Mixer** lets you modify a colour channel using a mix of the current colour channels.

- **Gradient Map** lets you remap greyscale (lightness) information in the image to a selected gradient. The function replaces pixels of a given lightness in the original image with the corresponding colour value from the gradient spectrum.

- **Lens Filter** adjusts the colour balance for warming or cooling down your photos. It digitally mimics the placement of a filter on the front of your camera lens.

- **Threshold** creates a **monochromatic** (black and white) rendering. You can set the threshold, that is the lightness or grey value above which colours are inverted.

- **Equalize** evenly distributes the lightness levels between existing bottom (darkest) and top (lightest) values.

- **Negative Image** inverts the colours, giving the effect of a photographic negative.

- **Greyscale** reduces a colour picture to 256 shades of grey.

- **Posterize** produces a special effect by reducing the image to a limited number of colours.

Adjustment layers

Adjustment layers let you introduce any number of image adjustments experimentally. Instead of altering the image or layer directly, you allow yourself the option of revisiting the settings for a given adjustment as often as needed, while continuing to edit the image in other ways. If you later decide you don't even need an adjustment, you can simply remove it!

To create an adjustment layer, click the ▣ **New Adjustment Layer** button on the Layers tab (or choose the item from the Layers menu) and select the name of the adjustment to be applied; most of those listed above are available. Then, just as if you'd selected the same effect from the Image menu, you use a dialog to pick the settings to be applied. The image responds as if you'd used the Image menu—but if you look over on the Layers tab, you'll see a new adjustment layer has been inserted above the active layer.

Unlike other layer types (as described in Chapter 5), adjustment layers don't store content in the form of bitmap images, text, or shapes. Rather, each adjustment layer applies one effect to content on the layers below it. You can even combine multiple effects by stacking several adjustment layers.

To change the specific settings for an effect, simply double-click the adjustment layer's name in the list and then use the dialog again. Right-click to access conventional layer **Properties** such as name, blend mode or blend ranges. You can drag an adjustment layer up or down within the list to determine exactly which other layers are below and therefore affected by it.

👁 To see how the image looks without the effect, click the **Hide Layer** button next to the adjustment layer's name. If you decide to permanently remove the effect, you can delete the layer.

Let's look at applying an image adjustment as an example—in this case, adjusting brightness and contrast.

Adjusting brightness and contrast

For images that appear a little dark you can utilize the brightness/contrast image adjustment filters to improve it.

1. Click the 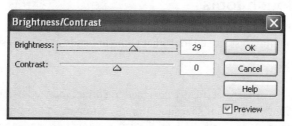 **New Adjustment Layer** button on the Layers tab.

2. Select **Brightness/Contrast...** from the flyout menu. This displays the Brightness/Contrast dialog.

3. Experiment with the **Brightness** and **Contrast** sliders. Each time you change a slider setting, the image updates. Alternatively, you can type values directly into the fields at the right.

Although you may not achieve perfection with just the Brightness/Contrast adjustment, try to obtain solid "bottom" and "top" (shadow and highlight) regions without obscuring details or washing out the image. The Brightness slider tends to move all the tones in the image one way or the other; Contrast compresses or expands the spread between bottom and top. Try different values—but remember that monitor settings and room lighting can make a difference.

4. When the picture looks better, click **OK**.

Besides Brightness/Contrast, the PhotoPlus Image menu affords a number of functions you can apply to correct shadow/highlight values in an image. **Adjust>AutoLevels** or **Adjust>AutoContrast** may do the job in one go; if not, you can use **Adjust>Levels...** or **Adjust>Shadow/Highlight/Midtone....** (See online help for details.)

Correcting Images

The focus has so far been on making adjustments to an image's colour, shadows, highlights and midtones. However, there are other adjustments that may be needed to correct that near-perfect photograph. If you've been snapping with your digital camera or maybe just scanned a photograph, at some point you may need to call on PhotoPlus's powerful photo-correction tools to fix some unforeseen problems.

For photo-correction, several methods can be adopted. You can use:

- **Image Adjustments**. As previously discussed, for applying adjustments to a selection or layer independently of each other.

- **Retouch brush-based tools**: Red Eye, Smudge, Blur, Sharpen, Dodge/Burn (for exposure control), Sponge (for saturation control), Scratch Remover.

- **QuickFix Studio**: For making cumulative image adjustments from within a studio environment.

Using the Retouch tools

The Retouch Tools flyout (Tools toolbar) includes an assortment of comparatively simple brush-based tools that come in handy at various stages of photo editing.

The **Red Eye Tool** is specifically designed to correct the "red eye" phenomenon common in colour snapshots. Simply zoom in on the subject's pupil and, with the tool selected, click on the red eye area to remove the unwanted tint. Alternatively, you can drag an ellipse around the area with your mouse cursor—releasing the mouse button removes the red eye effect.

Smudging may sound silly, but the **Smudge Tool** can be quite useful for blending pixels the way an artist might hand-blend pastels. Along with the Clone Tool, it's useful for blending together separate images in collage work, where seamless stitching is essential.

To use the tool, select it and drag to pick up colour from the initial click point and "push" it in the direction of the brush stroke. Short back-and-forth strokes work well to blend edges. Smudge tool properties are the same as for the Paintbrush, except that there's no Fade setting.

- Using an image with multiple lines or sharp edges, try using the tool to smear a line or edge outward, or create a mix of two colours (using a semi-transparent setting). Experiment with the effects of both a hard-edge and a soft-edge brush tip. For best results when using extended strokes, set the brush tip's Spacing property to 1.

The **Blur Tool** reduces contrast under the brush, softening edges without smearing colours the way the Smudge Tool would. To apply the same effect to a selected region or the active layer, use the **Effects>Blur>Blur...** command.

The **Sharpen Tool** has the opposite effect, increasing contrast under the brush to accentuate the appearance of sharpness. Use options in **Effects>Sharpen** to sharpen an entire selection or layer.

The **Dodge** and **Burn** tools complement one another. In the darkroom, while exposing a print from a projected negative, photographers have typically used their hands (or specially shaped tools) as needed to vary the amount of light reaching specific parts of the print. Dodging means reducing the exposure, while burning-in means increasing it. The PhotoPlus tools work the same way: brushing with the Dodge Tool lightens pixels, while the Burn Tool darkens the area under the brush.

The **Sponge Tool** changes the colour saturation of an area, either increasing or decreasing it depending on the Context toolbar setting. Lowering the Flow value produces a more subtle effect.

The **Scratch Remover Tool**, as its name implies, is effective at filling in small gaps or dropouts in an image. Like the Clone Tool it "picks up" values from one place and puts them down in another. You **Shift**-click to define a pickup point, then brush elsewhere to lay down paint. Unlike the Clone Tool, the Scratch Remover attempts to maintain colour values in the region under repair. As soon as you stop brushing, you'll see the surrounding colour magically flow into the repaired region!

The **Replace Colour Tool** provides a quick way to replace background colour with foreground colour. Use the Colour Picker to define foreground and background colour, then paint with foreground colour to replace any pixels matching that background colour. It's possible to control the extent of colour replacement with the Context toolbar's **Tolerance** setting.

Using QuickFix Studio

The purpose of the QuickFix Studio is to provide an image adjustment environment within PhotoPlus which simplifies the often complicated process of image correction. You can consider QuickFix Studio as the image adjustment equivalent of PhotoPlus's Filter Gallery, which instead concentrates on applying and managing special effects (we'll cover the Filter Gallery soon).

An important feature in QuickFix Studio is the ability to cumulatively apply filters (like the filter gallery)—normally you won't need to apply every correction filter available but a combination of several filters is more likely.

To launch **QuickFix Studio**, click the button on the Photo Studio toolbar (or select it from the Effects menu).

Let's get familiar with the QuickFix Studio's interface.. the example used is of a wide-angle photo of an interesting building (the unwanted barrel distortion effect is being removed).

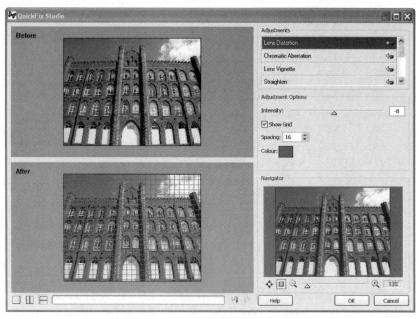

Available adjustments are listed to the right of the full-screen preview window (Lens Distortion is currently selected). Click on an **Adjustment** in the list then alter its **Adjustment Options** displayed below the adjustment list. Depending on the type of adjustment, a selection of sliders, check boxes, and drop-down menus (even enter absolute values into available input boxes) can be modified. Whatever settings are changed, the image will be adjusted automatically to reflect the new settings—don't be afraid to experiment as you can always click the ↩ **Reset** button next to the adjustment name to remove the adjustment completely.

Here's a quick overview of all the adjustments hosted in QuickFix Studio:

- **Lens Distortion**—fixes barreling and pincushion distortion with the help of an optional alignment grid (with changeable size and colour; see previous example).

- **Chromatic Aberration**—reduces red/cyan or blue/yellow fringing on object edges.

- **Lens Vignette**—removes darkening in photo corners.

- **Straighten**—re-aligns slightly or wildly crooked photos by resetting the image's horizon! Uses an optional alignment grid (with changeable size and colour).

- **Crop**—retains a print-size portion of your image while discarding the remainder. Great for home printing, then framing. Optionally, size an unconstrained selection area to crop.

- **Red Eye**—removes the dreaded red eye effect from friend's and family's eyes—commonly encountered with flash photography.

- **Brightness & Contrast**—simple adjustments to a photo's brightness, contrast, shadows, and highlights.

- **Colour**—"cool down" or "warm up" your photo by adjusting white balance (combination of temperature and tint). Colour saturation can also be altered.

- **Greyscale**—Intelligent greyscaling with red, green or blue channel adjustment.

- **Sharpen**—makes your image sharper at image edges—great for improving image quality after other adjustments have been made.

Some adjustments can also be applied independently from the Effects menu. See the PhotoPlus Help index for a closer look at each adjustment.

The order in which the above adjustments are applied is not critical but a typical photo-correction operation may involve the following steps chronologically.

1. Straighten

2. Crop

3. Adjust Shadows/Highlights (from Brightness &.Contrast)

4. Adjust Colour (warm up/down)

5. Sharpen

To make life as easy as possible while applying adjustments, a range of supporting tools are available within QuickFix Studio:

- You can **Zoom** into specific areas of your **Before** or **After** previews when the **Alt** key is pressed—left- and right-clicking will zoom in and out in set increments, respectively, or you can zoom in to a specific area by dragging a marquee around an item of interest.

- **Pan** around both previews simultaneously. Use the default hand cursor to drag around a zoomed-in portion of your photo.

- The Navigator window in the lower right-hand corner of the gallery, works identically to the Navigator tab (see p. 30)—it's perfect for quickly seeing different parts of the image and changing the zoom view. When zoomed in, simply drag the red view box over objects of interest, while optionally using the **Zoom to Fit** and **Actual Size** buttons, or the zoom slider, to change the viewable area.

- QuickFix Photo will allow you to alter the preview display mode—use the buttons at the bottom left of the preview window, i.e.

  - Shows a left/right **before/after** display (for portrait photos).

  - Shows a top/bottom **before/after** display (for landscape photos).

  - Shows a single image preview.

If you don't like your last made adjustment you can take advantage of the **Undo** and **Redo** buttons (in fact the undo is unlimited). The **Reset** button also reverts the image back to its original pre-adjusted state.

Now you have an understanding of how to correct your photos, the next step is to take your photos to a new level by applying stunning special effect filters!

Applying Special Effects

Using Effect Filters

PhotoPlus comes equipped with filters that can be used to give your photos some surprisingly powerful and diverse effects. As with image adjustment filters you can use these effects to improve the image—for example **Sharpen>Unsharp Mask** for crisper detail or **Noise>Median** to remove digital camera artefacts—but more often the emphasis here is on PhotoPlus's "creative" possibilities.

Creative filters include filters for blur (including the awesome **Depth of Field** blur and **Average Colour**), distortion, edge, noise, render, emboss, mosaic.. to name only a few types. As an example, the impressive **Paper Cutouts** filter (no need for scissors!) translates your image into a Matisse-style "collage" of cutouts of different size, shape and colour (see the following Filter Gallery example).

A large number of filters can be directly applied not only individually but cumulatively—each filter customizable. See the *Being Creative - Applying special effects* section of the How To tab (see p. 27) for a visual indication of what each effect can do.

PhotoPlus also lets you place industry-standard Photoshop plug-in filters in a Plugins folder and access them from the Effects menu. You can even define your own custom filters (see online help for details).

Using the Filter Gallery

- To access an effect, choose the Effects menu and select one of the effect group names (e.g., Distort), then select a filter name. This displays the selected filter in the **Filter Gallery**.
  OR

- ▦ To launch the **Filter Gallery** with no filter loaded, click the button on the Photo Studio toolbar (or select from the Effects menu).

The gallery offers a one-stop shop for applying your filters–all supported by an impressively large preview window that updates as you adjust an effects' sliders or enter new values. To see a different part of the image, drag it with the hand cursor. Select a magnification level from the lower-left drop-down menu, drag on the preview window to zoom to the drawn marquee selection area, or use the **Alt** key with left- or right-clicking to zoom in/out in increments!

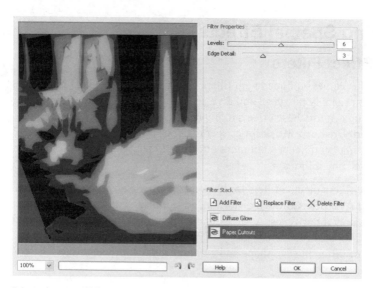

It's quite possible to apply several effects to the same image within the Filter Gallery, and, depending on the order in which they are applied, to end up with a different final result.

Adding a Filter

Adding a filter is as easy as selecting the **Add Filter** button and choosing a filter from the flyout menu. As soon as your filter is selected it is added to a filter stack where additional filters can be added and built up by using the same method. Any filter can be switched on/off, deleted or reordered in this list. The order in which filters appear in the filter list may produce very different results—don't worry, if you're not happy with your current filter order—PhotoPlus lets you drag and drop your filters into any position in the stack.

Filters are applied in the same way that layers are applied, i.e. the first filter applied always appears at the bottom of the list and is applied to the photo first. In the above example, the Paper Cutouts filter is applied first, then Diffuse Glow next.

If at any point you wish to swap one filter for another, while retaining the current filter list, simply select the filter to be removed, select **Replace Filter** and pick the replacement filter from the flyout menu.

Use the **Undo** button to undo the most recent change to the filter (or the **Redo** button to re-apply the change).

Switching on/off Filters

In the same way in which a layer's contents can be made invisible, the eye icon can make a filter's effect invisible (closed eye) or visible (open eye). As an example, a click on the Paper Cutout closed eye icon will make the filter visible like the Diffuse Glow filter.

Modifying a Filter

The properties of any selected filter will be displayed in the Filter properties box—you can alter and experiment with these at any time. For example, in the Filter Gallery dialog, the properties of the selected Paper Cutout filter, i.e. Levels or Edge Detail, can be adjusted by using the sliders or value input boxes.

Reordering Filters

Filters can be moved around the filter list to change the order in which they are applied to the photo. Drag a filter name to another position in the list while holding down the mouse button. A red line indicates the new position in which the filter will be place if the mouse button is released.

Instant Artist Effects

Instant Artist will bring your artistic side out—creating your own masterpieces by picking from a variety of classic painting styles (with no paint splashes!). The tool will transform your image in a single-click. Classic styles include **Expressionist, Impressionist, Oil, Old Master**, and many others.. more abstract styles are available such as **Munchist** and **Van Gogh**.

- To launch **Instant Artist**, either click the button on the Photo Studio toolbar or select the option from the Effects menu.

Either way, selecting a painting style from the left-hand menu will give you some fantastic quickly won artistic effects—plus hours of fun! Simply adjust the style properties underneath the preview window to your requirements.

For illustrated details, search for "Instant Artist" in the PhotoPlus Help index.

2D/3D Effects

Finally, the wide range of PhotoPlus 2D and 3D **layer effects** should be mentioned, available from the **Effects>Effects** option on the Layers menu. Unlike image adjustments and Effects menu manipulations, layer effects don't directly change image pixels—they work like mathematical "lenses" that transform how a layer's bitmap appears. Since the settings are independent, you can adjust them *ad infinitum* until you get the result you want!

For more details, see Layer effects on p. 112.

Tutorial Resources

For more experience with the tools and techniques covered in this chapter, we recommend these PDF-based tutorials available from PhotoPlus's Help menu:

Try this tutorial...	For practice with these tools and techniques...
Making Basic Image Corrections	Red Eye Tool, colour balance, brightness and contrast, levels and curves adjustments, adjustment layers
Repairing and Restoring Photographs	Clone Tool, layers, Paint to Select mode, Gradient Fill Tool, curves adjustments, Unsharp mask
Colouring Black and White Images	Adding colour to a greyscale image
Creating Oil Painting Effect	Median Cut, Edge Enhance image filters; Export Optimizer
Sharpening Images	Sharpen, Sharpen More, Sharpen Edges, and Unsharp Mask
Making Contrast Adjustments	Brightness/Contrast, Unsharp Mask, local contrast enhancement, Shadow/Highlight/Midtone adjustments
Creating Macros and Batch Processing	Resize multiple images using a macro with batch processing
Creating an Infrared Effect	Adjustment layers, Gaussian Blur, Channels tab
Creating Dramatic Lighting Effects	Lighting Effects, multiple light sources
Creating Modern Art	Gradient Fill Tool, Blend Modes

Working with Paint, Shapes, and Text

The previous chapter described a variety of ways of working with existing images—especially photographs, and usually on a single layer. Now it's time to look at creating elements from scratch, using the range of PhotoPlus paint and text tools. Perhaps you need to add text to a photo, or perhaps you're starting out with a blank canvas and want to try some interesting graphic shapes and colour combinations for a logo.

Whatever your creative goals, all of the functions described in this chapter can be applied to photographic images or images opened from a file as well as to new work!

Choosing Colours

At any given time, PhotoPlus allows you to work with any two colours—called the **foreground** colour and the **background** colour. These are always visible as two swatches on the **Colour tab** indicated below (ringed).

In the example opposite, the foreground colour is set to orange (RGB 255:97:38) and the background colour to white. (Don't confuse the "background colour" with the "Background layer"—there's absolutely no connection!).

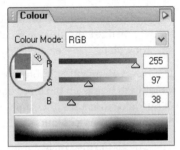

Here are some things to remember about how these colours are used:

• Cutting, deleting, or erasing an area on the Background layer exposes the background colour. On other layers, removing an area exposes transparency.

• To swap foreground and background colours, click the ⬧ double arrow at the top right of the Colour tab swatches. To reset the colours to black and white, click the black and white mini-swatch just to the bottom left.

There are a several simple ways to set the foreground or background colour.

One is to use the **Colour Pickup Tool** on the Tools toolbar. Left-click with the tool anywhere on an image to "pick up" the colour at that point as the new foreground colour, and right-click to define a new background colour. As a shortcut if you're working with one of the drawing tools (paintbrush, line, etc.), you can press the **Alt** key to switch temporarily to the Colour Pickup Tool. Release the key to switch back once you've left- or right-clicked to make a colour selection.

Another way is to use the Colour tab. To quickly select foreground or background colour, move the mouse pointer (dropper cursor) around the tab's **Colour Spectrum**. As you do so, a preview swatch pops up showing the colour at the cursor position. Left-click in the spectrum to set a new foreground colour, and right-click to set a new background colour. As a shortcut for white, drag up and off the top of the spectrum; for black, drag down and off.

Yet another method is to click either the foreground or the background swatch, then use the sliders or enter numeric values in the boxes to define a specific colour. The selected swatch updates instantly.

Double-clicking either a foreground or background colour swatch on the Colour tab brings up the more complex **Adjust Colour dialog**, which lets you define and store a set of custom colours interactively, using a colour wheel. See the "Choosing colours" topic in online help for details.

The Colour tab also makes it possible to set the working **Colour Mode** to any one of the following: **RGB** (Red, Green, Blue); **CMYK** (Cyan, Magenta, Yellow, Black); **HSL** (Hue, Saturation, Lightness); or **Greyscale**. Additionally, you can set the colour spectrum to display in normal RGB, Greyscale, or colours spread between the Foreground/Background colours (click the ▷ button on the tab). (For lots of useful terms and theory relating to colour definition and colour modes, see Chapter 8.)

If you repeatedly have to define the same colours from the Colour tab it may be more useful to save them as thumbnails to the **Swatches tab** (saving you a lot of effort) for future use. The tab hosts galleries of categorized colour thumbnails—by default you can store your own frequently used colours to the currently displayed gallery but you can also adopt pre-defined colours from a range of "themed" categories (e.g., Earth, Fruit, Pastel, and Web Safe).

- To add a colour to the Swatches tab, select the Colour Pickup Tool and hover over then click on a chosen colour (you'll notice the Colour tab's foreground colour swatch change).

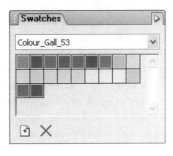

- Now that the colour is selected, a simple click of the **Add** button on the Swatches tab adds the foreground colour to the current gallery. You can jump between gallery categories by using the Categories drop-down menu (currently showing Colour_Gall_53).

- To apply a colour, select any gallery thumbnail then paint, draw, fill, etc.

Painting and Drawing

PhotoPlus's basic tools for painting and drawing are located, like the selection tools, on the Tools toolbar (initially at the left of the main window).

If you wish to display the related online help topic, choose the **Context Help** button and then click the Tools toolbar. (The same goes for any tab or toolbar.)

Using the basic Paintbrush Tool

The **Paintbrush Tool** is used for antialiased freehand drawing. Successful freehand drawing requires practice and a steady hand! You might find it easier if you use a graphics tablet, rather than a mouse.

- To paint a line using the Paintbrush Tool, select the tool from the Tools toolbar. When you move the Paintbrush Tool over the image the cursor will change into a paintbrush.

- Click and drag to draw a freehand line. Release the mouse button, then repeat to draw more lines.

- If you don't like what you drew, press **Ctrl+Z** to undo (but remember, this is all experimental—the more paint you get on the screen, the better!).

- Your lines appear in the currently selected foreground colour. To paint with the background colour, click the double arrow next to the Colour tab's swatches to switch the two colours. Try various techniques for selecting different foreground and background colours, as described earlier in the chapter.

- You might also try customizing the brush cursor, which ordinarily resembles the tool you've selected (in this case a paintbrush). Choose **Preferences...** from the File menu. On the General tab, switch to the **Brush Size** cursor and click **OK**. Now, the cursor is a small circle that graphically indicates the diameter of the current brush. Depending on the task at hand, you may find it more convenient to switch to this cursor—or perhaps the **Precise** cursor, a crosshair that leaves no doubt where the tool's "hotspot" is located.

Note that if there is currently a selection, the paint tool will only work *inside* the selected region. If you try to paint over the edge of a selection, the cursor will continue moving but the line will come to an abrupt halt at the edge of the selection. Or if you've forgotten that there's a selection (perhaps you hid the marquee) and the brush doesn't seem to work—you're probably just painting outside a selected region.

Choosing and customizing brush tips

All of the paint tools work in conjunction with the Brush Tip tab and/or Context toolbar, so let's see how they work with the basic Paintbrush Tool.

Brush tips determine the basic size and shape of the mark the brush tools make on-screen. The lines you've drawn so far with the Paintbrush Tool may be thick or thin, depending which brush is currently selected.

- Display the Brush Tip tab.

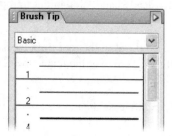

The tab displays a bevy of brush presets grouped into various categories, switchable via the drop-down list. Let's stick with the "Basic" gallery for now (as shown). Note that each sample clearly shows the brush tip and stroke; the number indicates the brush **diameter**. Other brush attributes aren't quite as obvious, as we'll see in a moment.

- Click the topmost sample for a single-pixel brush, and use it to draw a squiggly "pencil" line. (For straight lines, you can use a guide or the Straight Outline Tool, as described below.)

If you scroll down the gallery, you'll note that some brushes have hard edges, while others appear fuzzy, with soft edges. The **hardness** of a brush is expressed as a percentage of its full diameter. If less than 100%, the brush has a soft edge region within which the opacity of applied colour falls off gradually.

- To see what this means, try drawing a line with a medium-sized, hard-edge brush, and then switch to a soft-edge brush. You'll note the difference immediately.

Prior to painting, you can alter the brush tip's attributes by selecting your required brush preset from the Brush Tip tab and then adjusting attributes hosted on the Context toolbar. This leaves the brush presets unmodified.

To create a new brush preset, select a brush to be modified then change its Context toolbar's attributes. After this, use the ▷ **Tab Menu** button on the Brush Tip tab to create a new category (**Add Category...**) in which you can right-click and choose **New Brush...** Your new brush preset will appear in the category after naming.

You can also create a new brush from scratch by right-clicking in any user-defined brush category, delete a brush, or (when using the Picture Brush Tool) import a Paint Shop Pro **picture tube**. To define a custom brush tip—for example using a special shape or extending a textured region—first select part of the image to be used as a custom brush (for best results, use a solid white background), then right-click on the tab and choose **Define Brush....**

Let's look at the Brush Context toolbar and its attributes in more detail.

Context toolbar

For the Paintbrush Tool, the properties for blend mode, opacity, brush characteristics, size, flow, and airbrush are available on the Brush Context toolbar, i.e.

The properties can be altered directly on the Context toolbar apart from the **Brush:** option. However, it can be double-clicked to reveal the Brush Options dialog.

Let's look at each option in turn...

- **Blend Mode** (set to Normal above) determines how the pixels the tool lays down interact with pixels already on the layer. It can be a bit complicated, with each mode comparing "old" and "new" pixels in terms of values like hue, lightness, and so on—see p. 110 for more information.

- **Opacity** is basically the same concept as "transparency"—they're just different ends of the same scale (0% opaque is 100% transparent). Thus a lower opacity value produces paint that's more transparent, with less effect on existing pixels on the layer—more of the underlying paint "shows through." A fully opaque stroke completely replaces all pixels in its path.

- **Brush** displays the Brush Options dialog in order to alter the brush tool's characteristics, also set from the Brush tip tab. See Brush characteristics below.

- **Size** sets the brush width.

- **Flow** controls the build up and rate of application (1% very slow rate to 100% applied immediately) of the brush colour onto your image, up to the current brush opacity setting. This simulates the effect of a pressure-sensitive pen.

- **Airbrush** mode behaves like a spray-can. Holding the tool over one spot with the left mouse button held down "sprays" more paint.

Take a few moments to experiment with varying the Opacity and Airbrush settings. With opacity, note how different settings affect the way the foreground colour gets painted over existing colour.

- Click "Layer 1" in the Layers tab and try painting on the upper, transparent layer. Using semi-transparent brush strokes, you'll begin to see how you can combine and overlap colours on different layers.

- Try airbrushing on both the Background and the standard (transparent) layer while varying properties, particularly opacity.

- If you're feeling adventurous, try out some different blend modes—but those are probably best left for more advanced explorations!

Brush characteristics

Select **Brush:** from the Context toolbar. In the dialog, attributes are grouped into seven categories: Size, Spacing, Shape, Opacity, Misc, Colour, and Texture. As you vary the settings, you can see the effect of each change in the lower preview window.

Each time you move the brush by a tiny interval, you're laying down one "dab" of paint. A line consists of multiple dabs joined together, and the **Spacing** settings let you spread these out to create dotted lines, with greater or lesser density depending on the "Dab Count" settings, and a "Scatter" option that distributes the dabs left and right of the path you're drawing. With these and several other tip attributes, the "Controller" setting lets you vary the results according to the Direction of your stroke, the Pressure you apply with a stylus input device, or at Random. The **Opacity** attribute adds a Fade controller option so your brush opacity falls off along the stroke in a specified number of steps. Use the **Misc** options Airbrush and Wet Edges for spray and wet edge effects. The **Colour** option sets the way PhotoPlus randomly recolours brush applications. The **Texture** attribute allows you to choose a pattern with which to modulate the painted strokes—for example, to simulate a textured surface like paper or canvas. See the Brush Tip tab's Visual Reference entry in online help for details on these and other available settings.

Before moving on, you may have noticed that all brush edges are always antialiased (producing a level of edge smoothing), even when brush hardness is set to a high value. To apply true hard edges without antialiasing, the **Pencil Tool**, hosted on the Tools toolbar's Brush flyout, can be used.

Painting with a pattern

You may have encountered the Patterns dialog, with its selection of pre-defined tiled bitmaps, while exploring the "Texture" attribute in the Brush Options dialog (click on the Texture rectangle). Using this attribute, you can customize a brush tip by picking a pattern that lets you simulate a particular surface texture while painting or airbrushing a colour. But that's just the start of what you can achieve with patterns in PhotoPlus!

The **Pattern Tool** lets you paint a pattern directly onto your canvas. In effect, it "clones" any pattern bitmap you've selected while providing the flexibility to paint wherever you wish, and control opacity, blend mode, and so on. Like the Clone Tool (discussed a few pages further on), the Pattern brush picks up pixels from a source—in this case, the bitmap pattern—and deposits them where you're drawing.

- Click the small down arrow next to the Clone flyout and choose the Pattern tool. Make sure (on the Brush Tip tab) you've got a fairly wide brush selected so the results will be more obvious.

- On the Context toolbar, click the **Pattern** sample to display the Patterns dialog. Right-click any of the thumbnails and note that you can select from various pattern categories (listed at the bottom of the popup menu). For now, choose **Patterns-Abstract** and select a pattern.

- Begin painting in a blank region and you'll see the pattern develop as you brush. The **Aligned** setting in the Context toolbar determines what happens each time you begin brushing in a new place. If checked, the pattern extends itself seamlessly with each new brush stroke; if unchecked, it begins again each time you click the mouse. (See Using the Clone Tool on p. 84).

  Note that with the Pattern Brush tool, the "pickup point" is always the upper-left pixel of the pattern bitmap.)

The built-in selection of patterns provides a useful starting point, but you can also create your own patterns from any selection—or even the whole image. Simply define the selection (if any) and choose **Create Pattern...** from the Edit menu. Select the category where you want to store the pattern, and a thumbnail will be deposited there, ready to brush on (or use as a brush tip texture or fill) at any time. As you've probably noticed, right-clicking the thumbnails in the Patterns dialog provides commands for editing the pattern categories... even for adding new patterns from stored bitmap files!

Patterns are versatile indeed... and we'll have even more to say about them later in this chapter (see Filling Regions on p. 90).

Using the Picture Brush tool

The  **Picture Brush Tool** works like a custom brush that sprays a series of pre-defined images at regular intervals as you drag. The Brush Tip tab lets you select from a variety of picture brushes in different categories.

- Choose the Picture Brush Tool and (on the Brush Tip tab) pick a brush tip to try out.

- Click in various places on your canvas. Then try dragging in a continuous line.

Note that the tool can be used either to "stamp" single images at specific points—by clicking and releasing the mouse button each time, as in the letter "S" above—or to lay out a continuous stream of pictures as you drag along a path. Either way, you can scale the size of the elements each brush produces, and control their spacing and sequencing. To do so, select and then right-click a brush name on the Brush Tip tab, and choose **Brush Options**.

The **Spacing** setting determines how closely the elements are packed together when you draw continuously. At the minimum setting of 1%, the brushed line resembles a tube of toothpaste! Higher settings increase the separation between each element.

The **Order** setting controls how the mini-images are laid down. Select **Sequentially** to apply the original element sequence repetitively along the line; **Randomly** to mix up the order of elements; or **By Direction** to place elements according to the line's local slope (in other words, the direction of your stroke determines which sequence appears).

How does the Picture Brush work? Each Picture Brush tip has its own stored master image where mini-images have been arranged in rows and columns. The **Rows** and **Columns** settings tell the tool how to partition each tip's master image—so you should leave these values intact.

By the way, note that if you right-click on any gallery sample, you can edit categories, access brush options, and import Paint Shop Pro picture tubes. With a bit of forethought, it's not difficult to lay out your own master images and from them create custom Picture Brush tips. (For details, see online help.)

Using the Eraser tools

Sometimes the rubber end of the pencil can be just as important to an artist as the pointed one. The three **Eraser tools** can replace an existing colour either with another colour or with degrees of transparency. This review of basic PhotoPlus painting and drawing techniques wouldn't be complete without considering how you can use these three tools—located on the Eraser Tools flyout—to enhance an image.

The standard **Eraser Tool** works very much like the Paintbrush, with the same range of Brush Tip and tool properties options. But instead, on the Background layer, erased pixels are replaced by (or mixed with) the current background colour. On other layers, they are "watered down" by adding transparency.

- To erase, select the tool from the flyout and drag over the image area. Try erasing and experiment with varying the Opacity setting on the Context toolbar. You'll see that erasing is by no means an all-or-nothing proposition. Some wonderfully creative effects are possible using a semi-transparent eraser to reduce the contribution of existing pixels to the overall image.

- Again, switch between the Background and standard layers to compare the results.

The **Background Eraser Tool** erases pixels that are similar to a sampled reference colour underlying the cursor crosshair. Hence it's perfect for painting out unwanted background colours. For example, you can use it to isolate objects or people photographed against a studio backdrop. You can set limits to be "Contiguous", "Discontiguous", or "Edge Detected" which helps to prevent erasure of similar pixels on the other side of the edge you're tracing. Try "Continual" sampling, which updates the reference colour as you drag, or "Once," which retains the colour sampled at the first click point; "Background Swatch" detects and erases the current background colour.

The **Flood Eraser Tool** fills a region with transparency, erasing pixels similar to the colour under the cursor when you first click. With both the Flood and Eraser tools, you can select a "Contiguous" effect to erase only pixels in the region around the initial sample point, or switch to a discontiguous effect to erase similar pixels anywhere in the image.

- Try both tools using different settings. Also, experiment with the Background Eraser's "Edge Detected" setting, which improves erasure on one side of a contrasting edge or line.

Warping and Cloning

In this section we'll look briefly at the Warp tools (Elastic, Pinch, Punch, Twirl, Thick/Thin, and Unwarp) and the Clone Tool. These will be useful once you've established the basic elements of an image—perhaps using multiple layers—and are ready to begin altering details and improving the overall image either creatively or technically.

Using the Warp tools

The entries on the **Warp Tools flyout** work as a group. Most of them shift pixels that the brush passes over, while the last one undoes the cumulative effects of the others. The actual amount of pixel displacement depends on the direction of brush movement, the brush tip, and the Context toolbar settings.

The **Elastic Warp Tool** shifts pixels in the direction of brush motion, hence the appearance of pulling or elasticity.

The **Pinch and Punch Tools** apply, respectively, a concave or convex spherical distortion under the brush. To apply this effect to a selection or layer, use **Effects>Distort>Pinch/Punch....**

The **Twirl Tools** produce a "spin art" effect—liquid paint on a surface revolving either clockwise or anti-clockwise around a central point. As with Pinch and Punch, you can apply either effect to a selection or layer using the **Effects>Distort>Twirl**.

The **Thick/Thin Warp Tool** shifts pixels 90° to the right of the brush direction, which has the effect of spreading or compressing edges along the stroke.

The **Unwarp Tool** quite simply lives up to its name. Drag the Unwarp brush across a warped region to restore its unwarped state.

Note that Unwarp only works as long as you're still using the Warp tools. Once you select some other tool that's not on the Warp Tools flyout, in effect your "warping session" is over. If you return to the flyout later, it's a new session—Unwarp will reset itself and forget any previous warping. Similarly, PhotoPlus treats all your operations during one warping session as a single, cumulative event; using the Undo command clears the whole session. As a safety measure, you might occasionally switch to a non-Warp tool in the midst of warping, just to record your work up to that point as a separate event.

On the Context toolbar (when a warp tool is selected), the **Opacity** setting determines the degree of warping or unwarping that takes place. The **Quality** setting relates to how carefully each tool calculates new pixel values while you're moving the brush, as opposed to using interpolation to speed things up. A higher Quality setting will produce better results on most systems, but try a lower setting if brush movement appears jerky. However powerful your system, it's a good idea to click the **Refine** button when you're done, to update the image using fully recalculated pixel values.

Using the Clone Tool

The **Clone Tool** is one of the most powerful weapons in the electronic artist's arsenal. Like all the preceding tools, it uses a brush, but it's really like two magic brushes locked together. While you trace or "pick up" an original drawing with one brush, the other draws ("puts down") an exact duplicate somewhere else.

When retouching, for example, you can use the Clone Tool to brush away skin blemishes by cloning some "good skin" over them, or remove an unwanted object from an image by extending some foliage to cover it.

To clone a region on the active or all layers, select the tool from the Tools toolbar's Clone flyout and set its properties in the Context toolbar. Then **Shift**-click where you want to begin copying; we'll call this the "pickup point." Click and begin dragging somewhere else—even in another image window—where you want to begin placing the copied pixels; let's term this the "putdown point." You'll see a crosshair cursor appear back at the pickup point. As you drag, pixels from the pickup region are cloned in the putdown region by the tool's brush tip. The crosshair and brush tip cursors move in sync. The result? A perfect copy.

> TIP: You'll get the best results if you clone a region that's well painted over, rather than just a thin line.

In addition to the usual settings, the Clone Tool has an **Aligned** option on the Context toolbar. This affects what happens if you use more than one brush stroke. There are two possibilities when you click to begin another stroke, as seen below.

Aligned:
The pickup point changes, staying
a fixed distance from the brush tip
on each subsequent stroke.

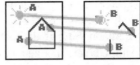

Non-aligned:
The pickup point stays in the same
place on each subsequent stroke.

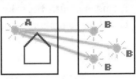

In the first case (called "aligned" because the two cursors remain in alignment), subsequent brush strokes extend the cloned region rather than producing multiple copies. In the second you begin cloning the same pixels all over again from the original pickup point.

The Pattern Tool and Scratch Remover Tool also feature this Aligned option. Once you're accustomed to painting with the Clone Tool, those more specialized tools will seem much more intuitive.

Up to now we've assumed that a single layer is being cloned, However, the Context toolbar hosts a **Use all layers** option which, when checked, will clone all layers (including Background, standard, Text and Shape layers together). When unchecked, only the active (selected) layer is cloned.

Creating and Editing Lines and Shapes

The tools we've described so far in this chapter have been for "pixel pushing"—manipulating the colour and/or transparency of the image content on the Background and standard layers. You may recall (from Chapter 2's Key Concepts) that PhotoPlus stores shapes separately, on special layers. It's a key distinction: lines and shapes in PhotoPlus are **vector** objects, as opposed to the **raster** or bitmap content that's stored on the regular pixel-based layers. So now we'll switch from covering the various **painting** tools to a different set of tools, used for **drawing** shapes.

The ▢▾ **QuickShape Tools** flyout features an assortment of tools for creating rectangles, ellipses, polygons, and other shapes.

The tools on the ▱▾ **Outline Tools** flyout let you draw outline shapes: skinny ones that serve as straight lines, plus outlines for variety.

Each of the drawing tools has its own creation and editing rules. Before we get to the differences, let's cover some things that all shape objects have in common. First of all, both QuickShapes and outline shapes occupy special **shape layers**, marked with an $\mathbb{S}$ symbol on the Layers tab. Each shape layer includes a **path thumbnail** representing the shape(s) on that layer. (We'll cover paths in more detail later; every shape has one). The path thumbnail must be selected to allow the path to be edited with the Shape Edit or Node Edit Tool.

Path thumbnail selected

Path thumbnail deselected

Assuming you're working on a non-shape layer when you create a shape, the new shape appears on a new shape layer. But what about the next shape you create? Shape layers can store more than one shape, and it's up to you where the next one will go.

This decision is made easy by use of the Context toolbar when the Outline or QuickShape tool is selected. The bar displays a series of **combination buttons** which determine the layer on which the shape will be placed and the relationship the new shape will have on any existing shapes on the same layer. Only one combination button can be active at any one time so it's important to ensure the correct button is active.

 New – adds the shape to a new shape layer.

 Add – adds the shape to the currently selected layer.

 Subtract – removes the overlap region when a new shape is drawn over existing shapes on the currently selected layer.

 Intersect – includes the intersection area only when a new shape is added onto existing selected shapes on the currently selected layer.

 Exclude - excludes the intersection area when a new shape is added onto existing selected shapes on the currently selected layer.

Did you notice the other icons on the Context toolbar? These icons let you choose whether your line or shape is added to a layer, created as a path, or is created as a filled bitmap, i.e.

Shape Layers - we use this to add a shape to a shape layers or create a new shape layer.

Paths - add your shape or line as a path. See later in this section for more information on paths.

Fill Bitmaps – creates a filled bitmap of the shape.

You can alter a shape layer's transparency using the Layers tab, or apply effects like bevel or drop shadow by choosing **Effects...** from the Layers menu (or via the **Add Layer Effects** button on the Layers tab). Painting tools and adjustment filters don't work on shape layers; you'll first need to convert the layer to a bitmap layer first (right-click the layer name and choose **Rasterize**).

To align or distribute shapes on different layers, select multiple layers with **Ctrl**-click or **Shift**-click then choose **Align** or **Distribute** options from the Layers menu. You can choose to align tops and bottoms, and so on.

QuickShapes

QuickShapes in PhotoPlus are pre-designed, filled contours that work just like the Adjustable Selection tools—you can instantly add rectangles, ellipses, polygons, and other shapes to your page, then adjust and vary them using control handles—for innumerable possibilities!

The **QuickShape Tools** flyout contains a wide variety of commonly used shapes, including boxes, ovals, arrows, polygons, and stars. Each shape has its own built-in "intelligent" properties, which you can use to customize the basic shape.

As you draw a QuickShape, it displays as an outline; hold down the **Ctrl** key while drawing to constrain the aspect ratio. Once drawn, the shape takes a Solid fill using the foreground colour (see p. 73). If you now switch to the Node Edit Tool, you can adjust the shape. The number of handles varies according to the shape; for example, the rectangle has just one control, the polygon has two, and the star has four.

To adjust a QuickShape, simply drag one of its handles (the tool changes to a "+" when it is above a handle).

Outline shapes

Earlier we noted that shape layers include a path thumbnail. The "path" is the outline around a shape, and although technically, QuickShapes have paths, too—the three Outline tools are genuine DIY (draw-it-yourself) path-drawing tools.

As we mentioned earlier, a straight line in PhotoPlus is just a very thin shape. To draw one, select the **Straight Outline Tool** from the Outline Tools flyout (Tools toolbar) and drag the tool on the image.

Hold down the **Shift** key while dragging to constrain the line to 15° angles.

The Context toolbar lets you set the **Weight** (thickness) of the drawn line, which is always **antialiased**. Antialiasing produces smooth edges by fixing "jaggies"—making the selection's edge pixels semi-transparent.

The **Freehand Outline Tool**, as its name implies, lets you draw a squiggly line (or a connected series, starting each segment from another's end point), then attach it back to itself to create a closed shape. Simply click and drag! The **Smoothness** setting on the Context toolbar evens out ragged contours automatically—useful if your hand shakes.

The **Curved Outline Tool** can produce complex combination curves and shapes in a highly controlled way.

- After choosing the tool, click and hold down the mouse button. An additional pair of handles appear, defining a pair of red **attractor nodes** that orbit the original click point as you continue to drag the mouse. What these nodes do is define the curvature of the line segment you're about to draw. The distance between attractors determines the depth of the resulting curved line.

- Release the mouse button, then click again where you want the first curved segment to end. To extend an existing path, repeat the process for each new end point. As with the Freehand Outline Tool, you can connect the curved outline back to its starting point. And you can switch between the two tools to construct a complex outline in a series of segments.

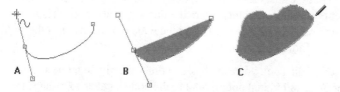

On a shape layer, PhotoPlus needs to treat each path as a closed shape, so it will automatically add a straight "closing segment" (as in the middle illustration above) even if you haven't joined the two end points. You can either leave the shape that way, or continue to draw segments until you yourself have officially closed it.

Editing shapes

The **Edit Tools** flyout includes two tools custom-made for editing QuickShapes and outline shapes. To edit either kind, first select its layer and make sure the layer's path thumbnail is selected.

You can use the Move Tool to reposition the shapes on a layer as a group, but the Shape Edit Tool does much more. In fact, it applies the move, resize, scale, skew, and rotation functions of the Deform tool to individual shapes on a shape layer. While the Shape Edit Tool is active, you can also use the combination buttons on the Context toolbar to reset how a selected shape (other than the first one you created on the layer) interacts with other shapes.

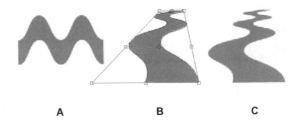

A   B   C

The illustration above shows a cool feature of QuickShapes: you can deform one with the Shape Edit Tool (in B, changing A's wave into a "road") and it will still remain adjustable with the **Node Edit Tool**! If you look closely at C, you'll note we've added an extra bend to the "road" after the deformation!

Besides being useful with QuickShapes, the Node Edit Tool really comes into its own with outline shapes. What is an outline, anyway? It's a collection of **line segments** and **nodes** (points where the line segments meet). There are three different node types (see p. 54), and the node type determines the slope and curvature of adjoining segments.

With the Node Edit Tool, you can click and drag directly on a line segment, drag one or more individual nodes, or alter the node handles to reshape the outline. To add a new node, double-click on a line segment. To straighten a line, delete a node or change it from one type to another, use the set of buttons on the Context toolbar.

Filling Regions

Filling regions or layers is an alternative to brushing on colours or patterns. Making a selection prior to applying a fill, and setting appropriate options, can spell the difference between a humdrum effect and a spectacular one... so it's definitely worthwhile getting to know the wide variety of fill types available in PhotoPlus.

The **Fill Tools flyout** on the Tools toolbar includes two tools: **Flood Fill** and **Gradient Fill**. In addition, you can use the **Edit>Fill...** command to apply either a Colour or Pattern fill. As with the paint tools, if there is a selection, fill operations only affect pixels within the selected region. If you're operating on a shape or text layer, a single fill affects the interior of the object(s) on the layer.

Flood and pattern fills

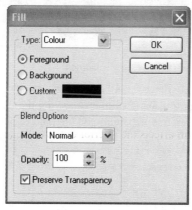 The **Flood Fill Tool** replaces an existing colour region with the foreground colour. The tool works only on standard layers, not with shape or text layers.

- Select the tool from the flyout, and set tolerance and layer fill options. Then just click with the tool where you want to start the flood! How large a region is "flooded" with the fill colour depends on the difference between the colour of the pixel you initially click and the colour of surrounding pixels.

You can use the Context toolbar to set a **tolerance** value—how much of a colour difference the tool looks for. With a low tolerance setting, the tool gives up easily and only fills pixels very close in colour to the one you click (a setting of 0 would fill only pixels of the same colour; 255 would fill all pixels). As the tolerance increases, so does the tool's effect on pixels further in colour from the original pixel, so a larger region is flooded.

Check **Antialias** to produce smoothing on the edges of any colour fill.

Check **Contiguous** to affect only pixels connected to the clicked pixel; uncheck to affect in-range pixels throughout the region.

If you wish to fill with a pattern—select Pattern rather than Foreground in the Fill drop-down box, click the adjacent Pattern box, and select a pattern from the **Patterns** dialog.

The **Edit>Fill...** command lets you flood-fill a region on a standard layer using any colour, not just the foreground colour. On the other hand, it's strictly a solid colour flood without the subtleties of the tool properties noted above. Simply choose the command to display the Fill dialog.

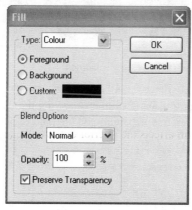

For a flood fill, set the Type to "Colour," and specify the blend mode and opacity of the fill. If you check **Preserve Transparency**, transparent areas will resist the flood colour; otherwise, everything in the selection or layer will be equally washed with the fill.

The other Type option in the Fill dialog is "Pattern." The blend options are the same, but in this mode instead of choosing a colour you can fill a region with any pattern stored in the Patterns dialog—including both the built-in bitmaps and any custom patterns you've created. (See Painting with a pattern on p. 80). Click the pattern sample in the Fill dialog to bring up the gallery of pattern thumbnails, then right-click any thumbnail to choose a category from the bottom of the list (you can also add, edit and delete pattern categories from here).

Gradient fills

Whereas solid fills use a single colour, all **gradient fills** in PhotoPlus utilize at least two "key" colours, with a spread of hues in between each key colour, creating a "spectrum" effect. You can fine-tune the actual spread of colour between pairs of key colours. Likewise, a gradient fill in PhotoPlus can have either solid transparency—one level of opacity, like 50% or 100%, across its entire range—or variable transparency, with at least two "key" opacity levels and a spread of values in between. (Remember that opacity is simply an inverse way of expressing transparency.)

The **Gradient Fill Tool** lets you apply both colour and/or transparency fills directly to a layer. Five types of fill (**Solid, Linear, Radial, Conical**, and **Square**) are available. Technically, a Solid fill is different (it uses just one colour)—but in practice you can also achieve a unicolour effect using a gradient fill.

| Solid | Linear | Radial | Conical | Square |

Applying a gradient fill on any kind of layer entails selecting one of the fill types, editing the fill colours and/or transparency, then applying the fill. However, gradient fills behave differently depending on the kind of layer you're working on.

On standard and Background layers, the tool creates a "spectrum" effect, filling the active layer or selection with colours spreading between the current foreground and background colours. The fill is applied rather like a coat of spray paint over existing pixels on the layer; colour values in the fill gradient interact with the existing pixels to produce new values. In other words, once you've applied the fill, you can't go back and edit it (except by undoing it and trying again). Transparency works in a comparable way, affecting how much the paint you apply is "thinned." At full opacity, the fill completely obscures pixels underneath.

Because text and shapes are vector objects in PhotoPlus, the Gradient Fill Tool is even more powerful on these layers—the fill's colour and transparency properties remain editable. Note that the Gradient Fill Tool doubles on these layers as a solid fill tool; the Flood Fill Tool doesn't work with text or shapes.

When first drawn, a shape takes a Solid fill using the foreground colour. To edit the colour or switch to a different fill type, either double-click the layer name or choose the Gradient Fill Tool and use the Context toolbar. Either option lets you choose a fill type, and/or click the colour (or gradient) sample to edit the fill. Gradient fills incorporate both colour and transparency, and a single fill applies to all the shapes on a particular layer.

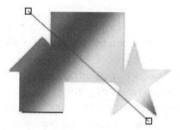

Once you've defined the fill, click with the tool where you want to start the fill and drag to the point where you want it to end. On shape and text layers, the **fill path** (the line in the illustration above) remains visible even after you've applied the fill, and you can adjust the fill's placement after the fact by dragging the fill path's end nodes with the Gradient Fill Tool.

The above example shows a gradient fill applied across three QuickShapes present on the same layer.

Editing a gradient fill

As mentioned above, to define a fill before you apply it, or to change it after the fact on a shape or text layer, you simply click the gradient sample on the Context toolbar. The PhotoPlus **Gradient** dialog appears whenever you're editing a gradient fill, and lets you adjust the fill's colour and/or transparency spreads. Its central feature is a sample window with a spectrum showing both colour and transparency.

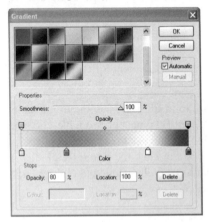

The little house-shaped pointers above and below the spectrum are the key to making changes in the dialog. Each pointer marks a **stop** where a **spread** of either opacity or colour begins and ends. To vary the colour gradient, you'll use the lower pointers, which show **key colours**. To vary the transparency gradient, you'll work with the upper set of pointers, which use greyscale values to represent key **opacity** levels (white = 100% opaque). In the example shown, the gradient has three colour spreads, and one opacity spread (actually uniform opacity, with 80% at each end). As you can see, the position of the pointers corresponds to transition points in each gradient.

Whether you're adjusting the fill's colour or its opacity properties, the same basic steps are involved. To make life very simple, you can begin by selecting a preset fill from the gallery. Right-click the gallery to select a different category, or add/delete your own fills or categories. A series of gradient categories are also available to choose from (e.g., Candy, Greens, etc.).

Add Item
Delete Item

Add Category...
Edit Category...
Delete Category

✔ [Default]
Blues
Candy
Greens
Masks

For more complex banding in a gradient, add one or more stops to define new key values and spreads. Click at the position where you want to place the new stop—either just above the spectrum to add a transparency stop or just below it for to add a colour stop. A new pointer appears, using an intermediate value. (The tip of a selected pointer is black; unselected pointers have grey tips.)

To change a key colour, select its stop and click the **Colour** box (or just double-click the pointer) to display the Adjust Colour dialog, then select the new colour. To change a key opacity value, select the stop and type a percentage into the **Opacity** box. To adjust the length of a spread, move an intermediate stop by dragging its pointer to a new position along the spectrum. You can also select the pointer, then type a number into the **Location** box. To delete a stop you've added, click to select its pointer and click the appropriate **Delete** button (or press the **Delete** key).

The diamond-shaped markers that may appear between stops let you adjust the spread of values between the two stops. Initially, values are graduated evenly from one stop to the next. To change the value distribution between adjacent stops, simply drag the intermediate marker. Adjust the **Smoothness** slider for more even transitions between bands in a multicolour fill. Finally, click **OK** to accept changes.

Working with Paths

Paths are basically outlines. As such, every filled shape you draw has a path—namely the outline that defines it. We noted that each shape layer has its own path thumbnail next to the layer name, representing the shape(s) that reside on that layer. But PhotoPlus also lets you work with **independent paths**: outlines that don't reside on any particular layer, but which are created separately and can be applied in various ways to any layer.

What are paths good for? Consider the precision and editability of vector-based drawing and apply it to the concept of a selection. Now think of all the ways that selections can be used (and reused). In PhotoPlus, selections and paths are interchangeable.

The **Paths** tab provides a special window for working with independent paths. You can create a path which will show its name and **path outline** as a thumbnail within the tab after creating it from a drawn QuickShape, outline or any current selection. If needed, you can enlarge the outline thumbnail from the **Tab Menu** button at the top-right of the tab.

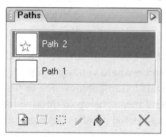

In Path 2's thumbnail above, the path outline produced from a drawn Quick Star is shown. Once you've got a path outline, you can still reshape it with the same Edit tools you'd use for shapes, and convert it to a selection. You can even **stroke** a path—that is, trace it onto a bitmap layer using the current brush. Paths are saved along with the image whenever you use the .SPP format.

- To create a path outline, select a QuickShape and/or outline tool, then select the **Paths** icon from the Context toolbar. You can then draw the shape as a path outline automatically. (See Creating and editing lines and shapes on p. 85). Note how a new path either appears in the Paths tab, or an existing path is altered—this depends on the combination button settings (also on the Context toolbar). Alternatively, you can create a path from the current selection simply by clicking the **Selection to Path** button on the Paths tab. This method creates a new path automatically and lets you choose a **Smoothness** setting to even out jagged selections, if you wish. Either way, you'll end up with an unfilled shape on the path. To duplicate, delete, or rename a path, right-click it and choose from the menu. (You can also double-click a path to rename it.)

- To edit a path outline, you use the same Node Edit and Shape Edit tools described earlier for shape-editing. Simply select any path in the Paths tab and then select the required tool. For the Node Edit Tool, clicking on the path lets you modify a QuickShape's shape by dragging its handles, or for a line you can move nodes to change the path shape. For the Shape Edit Tool, clicking a shape, line or selection lets you drag the displayed bounding box handles in any direction to move, resize, reshape, rotate, and skew the path. You can also flip a path outline either horizontally or vertically. Use the **Flip Horizontally>Path** or **Flip Vertically>Path** option from the Image menu, respectively.

- To create a selection from a path, use the Layers tab to select the target Background or standard layer, and on the Paths tab, select the path from which you want to make the selection. Click the **Path to Selection** button. A dialog appears with various options for the new selection: feathering, antialiasing, and combination. (See Making Selections on p. 41.) Click **OK** and the selection marquee appears on the target layer.

Stroking a path is a convenient way of creating painted lines or unfilled shapes without having to draw them directly. First select the target layer and source path. Choose a brush tool (such as the Paintbrush or Picture Brush) and set Colour, Brush Tip, and Context toolbar properties. Make sure the path is positioned where you want it, then click the **Stroke Path** button on the Paths tab.

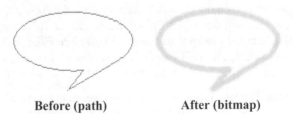

Before (path)   **After (bitmap)**

The **Fill Path** option lets you fill any created path with the current foreground colour.

Working with Text

Use the **Text Tools flyout** on the Tools toolbar to select from two text tools—one for entering solid, colourful text on a new layer, and the other for creating a selection in the shape of text with which to manipulate content on an existing layer.

- **A** To create new solid text on a new layer, choose the standard **Text Tool** from the flyout and then either:

  - Click on your image with the text cursor to set where you want to insert text. The text attributes (font, point size, bold/italic/underline, alignment, antialias and colour) set on the Text Context toolbar prior to clicking will be applied.
    OR
    Drag across the page to size your text according to requirements. Release the mouse button to set the point size.

- Type your text directly on the page.

- To edit text, select all or part of the text and format using the options on the Text Context toolbar shown above your image. Semi-transparent edges to the characters are applied when the **Antialias** box is checked. (Antialiasing is generally recommended with text sizes 14pt or larger.)

To edit your text's solid colour, select all or a portion of your text, click the colour swatch on the Context toolbar and use the **Adjust Colour** dialog. (For details on using the Adjust Colour dialog, see the "Choosing colours" topic in online help.). To swap to a gradient fill, use **Edit Fill...** (right-click on the Text layer) to change to a **Fill Type** of Linear, Radial, Conical, or Square—click on the gradient swatch and define a gradient fill from the dialog.

The text appears on a new transparent layer in the image. You can now use the Move Tool or other tools and commands to manipulate it, just like the contents of any layer.

The Layers tab designates **text layers** with a T symbol. Like shapes (as discussed earlier), solid text in PhotoPlus is *editable*: as long as it remains on a separate text layer, you can retype it or change its properties at a later date. To edit existing text, select the layer and—using the standard Text Tool—move the cursor over the text until it changes to an I-beam, then click on or drag to select areas of text—this lets you insert or overwrite selected text, respectively. Equally, you can select areas of text to change font, point size, and text colour.

In order to keep text editable, only one block of text can occupy a text layer, so various functions—such as paint tools, adjustment filters, or the **Paste Into Layer** command—are disabled on text layers. To convert any text layer to a standard layer, right-click on the layer name and choose **Rasterize** from the menu.

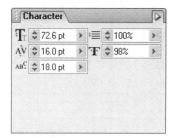

The **Character tab** provides a selection of tools for fine-tuning point size and the placement of text. Letter spacing (tracking), vertical character positioning (advance), leading and text width controls are hosted to apply more subtle effects to your text.

Text Selections

Text selections work like standard or adjustable selections, except that (you guessed it) they're shaped like text! This opens up a number of creative possibilities, such as using the text selections to "pick up" patterns or filling the region with unusual fills.

To create a text selection, choose the **Text Selection Tool** from the Text Tools flyout and click on the image to set a default text size or drag to your required point size. Type your text directly on the page and apply formatting just as you would if creating solid text. Once you're happy with the design of your text (and you want to make a selection of it), click the ✔ button on the Context toolbar—you'll now see a selection region on the active layer instead of the solid text. Now you can cut, copy, move, modify, and apply various effects to it, just as with the other types of selection.

Tutorial Resources

For more experience with the tools and techniques covered in this chapter, we recommend these PDF-based tutorials available from PhotoPlus's Help menu:

Try this tutorial...	For practice with these tools and techniques...
Selection Tools	Basic selection concepts
Colour Spaces	Colour Modes: Greyscale, RGB, HSL, and CMYK
Brush Tips and Tricks	Variable brushes using Brush Options
Using the Clone Tool	Clone Tool basics
Repairing and Restoring Photographs	Clone Tool for stitching images back together. Principles of image correction using Curves setting, Unsharp Mask, etc.

Using Layers
and Masks

Layers

If you're accustomed to thinking of pictures as flat illustrations in books, or photographic prints, the concept of **image layers** may take some getting used to. In fact, layers are hardly unique to electronic images. The emulsion of photographic film has separate layers, each sensitive to a different colour—and we've all noticed multiple-image depth effects like shop window reflections or mirrored interiors. There is still something magical about being able to build up an image in a series of planes, like sheets of electronic glass, each of which can vary in transparency and interact with the layers below to produce exciting new images and colours.

Kinds of layers

In a typical PhotoPlus image—for example, a photograph you've scanned in, a new picture file you've just created, or a standard bitmap file you've opened—there is one layer that behaves like a conventional "flat" image. This is called the **Background layer**, and you can think of it as having paint overlaid on an opaque, solid colour surface.

You can create any number of new layers in your image. Each new one appears on top of the rest, comprising a stack of layers that you can view and manipulate with the **Layers tab**. We call these additional layers **standard layers** (named Retouch and Paint1 opposite) to differentiate them from the Background layer. Standard layers behave like transparent sheets through which the underlying layers are visible.

In the previous chapter, we covered **shape layers** and **text layers**, which are specifically designed to keep objects (either shapes or text) separate from the other layers so that they remain editable. Chapter 3 described **adjustment layers**, which apply filter effects to lower layers. Refer back to the earlier sections for coverage of these special-purpose layers—here we are concerned mainly with the Background and standard layers.

A key thing to keep in mind is that pixels on the Background layer, once laid down, are fully opaque, while those on standard layers can vary in opacity (or transparency, which is really the same thing). That's because standard layers have a "master" Opacity setting that you can change at any time (with on-screen real-time preview), while the Background layer does not. A couple of examples will show how this rule is applied in PhotoPlus.

Suppose you are creating a new picture image. The New Image dialog provides three choices for Background: **White, Background Colour**, and **Transparent**. If you pick White or Background Colour, the Layers tab shows a single layer named "Background." If you pick Transparent, however, the single layer is named "Layer 1"—in this case, the image (typically an animation file) has no Background layer.

If you cut, delete, or move a selection on the Background layer, the "hole" that's left is filled with the current background colour (as shown on the Colour tab). The same operations on a standard layer leave a transparent hole.

Many standard operations, such as painting, selecting and moving, Clipboard actions, adjusting colours, applying effects, and so on, are possible on both the Background layer and standard layers.

Other operations, such as rearranging the order of layers in the stack, setting up different colour interactions (blend modes and blend ranges) between layers, varying layer opacity (transparency), masking, or creating animation frames, only work with standard layers.

Once an image has more than just a background layer, the layer information can only be preserved by saving the image in the native PhotoPlus (.SPP) format. Multiple layers are **merged** when you export an image to a standard "flat" bitmap format (e.g., .PNG). It's best to save your work-in-progress as .SPP files, and only export to a different file format as the final step.

Some standard operations can be applied to all layers by using the **Use All Layers** option from the Context toolbar.

Basic layer operations

To select a layer, click on its name in the Layers tab. The selected layer is now termed the **active layer**. (Note that "selecting" a layer doesn't imply selecting a region of pixels—that's a separate step, using tools described in Chapter 3.)

To create a new standard layer above the active layer, click the **New Layer** button on the Layers tab. To clone one or more active layers and their contents as new standard layers, right-click the selected layers then choose **Duplicate...** (or **Alt**-drag in the editing window with Move Tool selected). You can also copy the layer(s) to a new or currently opened image by the same process, or by dragging between documents. Dragging a file icon (or an active selection from any OLE server program) and dropping it onto the current window also creates a new layer from the dragged image.

To convert the Background layer to a standard (transparent) layer, right-click "Background" on the Layers tab and choose **Promote to Layer**. The layer's name changes from "Background" to "Layer <number>."

Select **New Layer Group** to create a group in which you can store layers which have some relationship to each other—some layers may only be related to a specific photo feature such that any changes to those layers will be restricted to the group's scope only. This gives greater control to enable changes to opacity, blend modes and hide/show layer settings for the group rather than individual layers.

Create a **New Adjustment Layer** to apply an image adjustment to a layer or group as described in Adjustment layers on p. 58.

The **Add Layer Mask** adds a mask to the currently selected layer or group as described in Masks on p. 117.

The **Add Layer Depth Map** creates a depth map for the selected layer or group.

Create a layer effect with the **Add Layer Effects** button. This can also be applied to a group.

To remove the active layer, click the **Delete** button on the Layers tab. (You can delete the Background layer, as long as it's not the last layer.)

To make a layer's contents visible or invisible, click the **Hide/Show Layer** button next to its name on the Layers tab. The icon switches between an open and closed eye.

Note that each layer's entry includes a preview thumbnail, which is visible at all times—especially useful if you're working with many similar layers, image fragments, and/or hidden layers.

A series of lock buttons exist above the layer entries in the Layers tab to prevent accidental modification of the active layer or group.

Lock Pixel Opacity—locks the opacity on the layer or group.

Lock Pixels—locks the opacity and colour on the layer or group.

Lock Layer Position—locks position of all objects on the layer or group.

Lock All—All of the above.

Manipulating layers

Control over layers means control over a great variety of creative possibilities. This section will review some of the manipulations you should know about.

Note that commands on the Image and Effects menus, such as colour adjustments and special effects, typically are applied to the current selection (if one exists). Otherwise they affect the active layer or group (the one currently selected in the Layers tab).

Let's firstly look at different selection methods before looking at how to manipulate layers.

Selecting layers

Any single layer can be selected with a single-click. However, for more advanced image editing a strong requirement is the ability to **select multiple layers** simultaneously. This allows manipulation of large portions of your project—and a lot of time saving by performing operations in "bulk".

Layer selection uses the same logic as used in selecting objects such as text and shapes. From the Layers tab, use **Ctrl**-click or **Shift**-click to select non-adjacent or adjacent multiple layers, respectively. Once selected, multiple layers can be moved, linked, aligned, duplicated, grouped, rearranged, hidden, merged and deleted simply and quickly. Interested in selecting all layers at the same time? Choose **Select All layers** from the Layers menu.

In addition, all layers that are part of a link can also be selected simultaneously—select one of the linked layers, then choose **Select Linked Layers** from the Layers menu.

Moving the contents of one or more layers

To move the contents of an active single layer or active multiple layers (plus any associated linked layers), make sure nothing is selected, then drag with the **Move Tool** or nudge with the keyboard arrows. Note that layer content moved in this way outside the image window (canvas area) survives—you can drag it back inside the window later if desired.

Linking layers

You can **link** one or more layers together to establish more permanent associations between particular layers. To do so, select multiple layers and choose **Link Layer** from the Layers menu. You'll notice a link icon appear next to each selected linked layer entry (the icon disappears on deselection of any linked layer). You can check to see which layers are linked together by selecting a linked layer—all layers linked to it will show the link icon. Once layers are linked, they remain so regardless of which layer in a linked group is active. To add a further layer to linked layers click on an existing link layer, choose the layer to be added via **Ctrl**-click or **Shift**-click and choose **Link Layers** (Layers menu). **Unlink Layers** disassociates a selected layer from other linked layers.

Aligning layers

To align selected layers with each other, select a range of layers and choose **Align** from the Layers menu, then select **Top**, **Vertical Centre**, **Bottom**, **Left**, **Horizontal Centre**, or **Right** from the submenu. Additionally, three or more objects on selected layers can be distributed equally by their **Top Edges**, **Left Edges**, **Right Edges** or **Bottom Edges**, or distributed to **Vertical Centre** or **Horizontal Centre**. Alternatively, use the same options as icons on the Context toolbar (with the Move Tool selected).

Deleting Layers

It is possible to delete one or more selected layers in the Layers tab simultaneously by selecting **Delete>Layers** from the Layers menu. Hidden layers can be deleted without prior selection by using **Delete>Hidden Layers**.

Clipboard operations involving layers

To copy (or cut) the contents of any selected background or standard layer to the Clipboard, select the layer and use the standard **Ctrl+C** or **Ctrl+X** commands.

If selected areas of a layer are to be cut then deleted pixels are replaced (on the Background layer) with the current background colour, or (on standard layers) with transparency.

You can paste the copied or cut layer (or selection) to a completely new image or to a new layer (in the same image) by respectively using the **Paste>As New Image** or **Paste>As New Layer** command on the Edit menu. Note that Text and Shape layers will become standard layers when pasted (and are no longer editable)—instead right-click your Text or Shape layer(s) and choose **Duplicate...** to copy such layers.

Rearranging layers in the stack

To move one or more layers up or down in the layer stack, select the layer(s) in the Layers tab and drag up or down. A red line "drop target" appears between layers as you drag. Drop the layer(s) on a target to relocate in the stack.

Another method is to select the layer(s) and choose **Arrange** from the Layers menu, then choose one of the following:

- **Bring to Top** places the layer(s) on the top of the stack.

- **Move Up** moves the layer(s) up one in the stack.

- **Move Down** moves the layer(s) down one in the stack.

- **Send to Bottom** places the layer(s) just above the Background layer (if present) in the stack.

Merging layers

Merging layers combines multiple layers (or groups) into one, decreasing the memory required to store the image. Once layers have been merged, they become a single layer and their previous contents are no longer separately editable.

To merge the active layer with the layer below it, right-click the active layer in the Layers tab and choose **Merge Down**. To merge just the currently visible layers into a single layer, choose **Merge Visible**. Again via right-click, merge currently selected layers into a single layer with **Merge Selected Layers**.

To merge all image layers into a single layer, right-click in the Layers tab and choose **Merge All**. This is called **flattening** the image because the result is a "flat" file with just a Background layer.

To copy the selection (or image, if there's no selection) to the Clipboard in flattened form without physically merging its layers, choose **Copy Merged** from the Edit menu.

Grouping Layers

For greater management and efficiency it is possible to place selected layers into a pre-defined group, created with the **New Layer Group** button in the Layers tab. Alternatively, you can select multiple layers and add them to a new unnamed group by selecting either **New Layer Group from Selected Layers...** or **Group Layers** on the Layers menu. There are many reasons why you might want to use groups in addition to layers. Here are a few...

- To create a self-contained group of layers which are all related, e.g. all the Text Layers used in your photo.

- To collect layers together which make up a specific photo feature.

- To make a mask or blend apply to only specific layers, i.e. those that contained within a group.

- To apply changes to a group that you would otherwise have to apply to each layer in turn—thus improving efficiency.

In reality a group is really just another layer but one which can store layers within itself. It's not surprising then that a group can have its own blend mode, opacity and blend ranges just like a layer. A group can also be merged, linked and made visible/invisible—or even grouped within another group.

The addition of one or more layers to a group is very simple. Select the layer(s) you want to add to the group and, while holding the mouse button down, drag onto the group name. The layer(s) will then appear indented under the group.

In the example, the highlighted "Text Additions" group contains two text layers called "Little House" and "copyright".

To remove a layer, drag the layer away from the group and drop it into an ungrouped area of the Layers tab. You can also use **Ungroup Layers** from the Layers menu if all layers are to be removed.

The **Merge Layer Group** option in the Layers menu can be used to merge all layers contained within a selected group.

Note that you cannot move the background layer to a group.

Blend Modes

You can think of **blend modes** as different ways of putting pixels together to create a resulting colour. In PhotoPlus, we've already encountered blend modes as a property of individual **tools** (Paintbrush, Clone, Eraser, Airbrush, Fill, Smudge, Shape, and Line), where the tool's blend mode determines how new colour pixels look when painting on top of existing pixels.

As a property of individual **layers,** a layer's blend mode determines the result of combining each pixel on that layer with those on layers below. (Because there are no layers below the Background layer, it can't have a blend mode.) Note that unlike working with paint tools, changing a layer's blend mode property doesn't actually alter the pixels on the layer. This means you can create different blend mode effects *after* creating the image content, then merge layers when you've achieved the result you want.

To set a layer's blend mode, select it on the Layers tab or in the Layer Properties dialog and choose from the drop-down list (shown at right).

For illustration of the individual blend modes, see "blend modes" in the PhotoPlus Help's index.

Blend Ranges

It's a good time to clear up the difference between Blend Modes and Blend Ranges. As we've seen, a Blend Mode can be associated with a tool or layer to produce different colour effects when pixels from each layer are painted on top of each other. Blend Ranges, a more advanced blending feature, differ in that they specify the range of colours on a current layer that is to be blended with the underlying layer—this is a simple include or exclude of tones or colours in the blending process. The **Layer Properties** dialog allows both the Blend Mode and Blend Ranges to be set for layers—take care when using these in conjunction with each other as they are a powerful combination.

The Blend Range can be set for Red, Green, Blue or Grey (shown) channels. The current layer and its underlying layer can be allocated a value from 0/0 to 255/255 each which represents the tonal or colour value—value pairs (e.g., 70\70 or 255\255) are set by moving the triangular sliders to the required value on the range selector. In the example above, the grey tones of value less than 70 are not included in the blend. This means that the colour of the underlying layers pixels is used instead (as there is no blending taking place).

For smoothing between colours included and excluded from the blend, it is possible to split the triangular sliders by dragging each half apart with the **Alt** key. This partial blending occurs linearly.

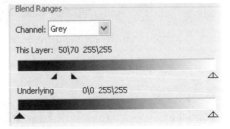

Extracting part of a layer

 The **Photo Studio toolbar** hosts an **Extract** feature which can speed the task of isolating one portion of a layer (you can also use **Edit>Extract...**). Using the special dialog, you simply brush an outline around the edges of the region you want to extract, then mark a "foreground" area to be retained—usually inside the outline. PhotoPlus applies sophisticated edge detection within the marked edge band, decides which pixels to keep, and turns the rest of the layer transparent, with variable blending along the edge. In preview mode, you can fine-tune and reapply the extraction settings, and manually touch up the image until the result is just right.

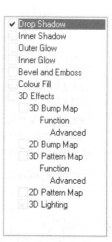

Instead of marking a foreground region, you can designate a specific "key" colour to which edge pixels can be compared. Similar pixels will be kept, and dissimilar pixels discarded. (See PhotoPlus Help for details.)

Layer Effects

Layer effects are creative effects that you can apply to the contents of standard (transparent) layers, text layers, or shape layers. Standard or **2D** layer effects like shadow, glow, bevel, and emboss are particularly well adapted to text, while **3D** layer effects create the impression of a textured surface. Because the Background layer doesn't support transparency, the effects are not available there. Another thing to keep in mind is that none of the layer effects will "do" anything to an empty layer—you'll need to have some colour there to see the difference they make!

✔ Drop Shadow
Inner Shadow
Outer Glow
Inner Glow
Bevel and Emboss
Colour Fill
3D Effects
3D Bump Map
Function
Advanced
2D Bump Map
3D Pattern Map
Function
Advanced
2D Pattern Map
3D Lighting

To apply an effect to the active layer, click the **Add Layer Effects** button on the Layers tab (or choose **Effects>Effects...** from the Layers menu). The **Layer Effects dialog** appears, with a branching checklist of available effects. As the checkbox format suggests, you can apply one or more effects to the same layer simply by checking boxes to switch them on individually.

Suppose we preview the settings for the 2D effect **Drop Shadow** shown as
enabled above.

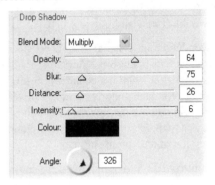

You can choose a **Blend Mode** to determine how the effect's colours interact
with image colours, and adjust Blur, Radius, Distance, and Intensity sliders (or
enter specific values) to change the total effect. In this particular dialog,
there's also an **Angle** dial that lets you control the direction of the cast
shadow, and a **Colour** swatch to change the base shadow colour.

Any effect applied to a layer can be temporarily hidden, as well as copied and
pasted, from the **Effects** option in the Layers menu or via right-click on the
Layers tab. **Clear Effects** (from menu or tab) removes the effect from the layer
permanently.

3D layer effects are just as easy to apply, but they're a bit more complex than
their 2D cousins. Actually, there's an easy way to get started with them:
simply display the **Instant Effects tab** and preview its gallery thumbnails.

In the tab you'll see a variety of remarkable
3D surface and texture presets grouped into
wide-ranging "themed" categories (e.g.,
Abstract, Wood, Metal, etc.). Click any
thumbnail to apply it to the active layer.
Use the **Shift** key to apply more than one
Instant Effect to existing layer effects
cumulatively. Assuming the layer has some
colour on it to start with, you'll see an
instant result!

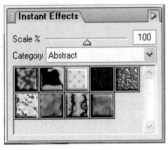

Depending on the size of your original image and what's depicted in it, you
may want to vary the **Scale** slider to reproportion the effect (for example, to
achieve a more realistic orange-peel texture). Having applied a preset effect,
you can now bring up the Layer Effects dialog and inspect the settings used in
the preset. The first thing you'll notice is that the **3D Effects** and **3D Lighting**

boxes will always be checked. The master settings of Blur and Depth make a great difference; you can click the "+" button to unlink them for independent adjustment. As for 3D Lighting, without a "light source" switched on, the depth information in the effect wouldn't be visible.

Another thing you'll probably wonder about is that all the 3D effects seem to have "map" in their name. So what is a map, anyway? Actually, it's the key to understanding how these effects work. Let's call it a channel of information overlaid on the image, storing values for each underlying image pixel. You can think of the layer as a picture printed on a flexible sheet, which is flat to start with. Each 3D effect employs a map that interacts with the underlying layer's image to create the impression of a textured surface.

Bump Maps superimpose depth information for a bumpy, peak-and-valley effect. Using the flexible sheet metaphor, the bump map adds up-and-down contours and the image "flexes" along with these bumps, like shrink-wrap, while a light from off to one side accentuates the contours. **Pattern Maps** contribute colour variations using a choice of blend modes and opacity, for realistic (or otherworldly!) depictions of wood grain, marbling, and blotches or striations of all kinds.

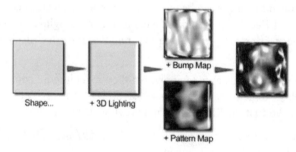

You'll notice that Bump Maps and Pattern Maps come in two varieties: "2D" and "3D." Don't be misled! These are all three-dimensional effects; the distinction has to do with how each one achieves its result. With the "3D" Bump Maps and Pattern Maps, you first pick a mathematical function. With the "2D" variants, you begin by selecting a bitmap from a gallery. The function-based maps include data about the interior of the "space," while the bitmap-based maps describe only surface characteristics. You'll see the distinction more clearly if you experiment with depth maps, as covered in the next section.

See PhotoPlus Help for extended technical coverage of the 3D layer effects. For now, just spend some time playing with them!

Depth Maps

Depth maps let you add remarkable 3D realism to ordinary images, with or without the use of 3D layer effects (as described above). A standard "flat" image, of course, has only two dimensions: X and Y, or width and height. Adding a depth map to a layer gives you an extra channel that stores information for a third (Z-axis or depth) dimension, in effect adding "volume" to the image. It's as if the original image acquires a surface with peaks and valleys—and you can play with the elevation of the landscape to achieve different visual results.

The depth map itself is a greyscale representation that uses lightness values to encode the Z-axis or "elevation" data, with 256 possible levels for each underlying image pixel. Lighter areas represent peaks and darker areas represent valleys. Here's a schematic view of how an imaginary 3D volume (the stack on the left) might be encoded as a depth map:

"Elevation" as lightness values...   ...on the depth map

The several levels of elevation on the stack translate or "map" directly to lightness values in the greyscale depth map on the right. What PhotoPlus can do is to take the depth map and translate it back into light-and-shadow information that appears (to us) as depth in an image... hence the illusion of three-dimensionality.

Typically, you'll begin by creating a new blank depth map on a layer, then modify it by painting or erasing directly on the map. Changes on the greyscale map layer produce the effect of highs and lows in the "surface." This kind of greyscale painting is not unlike using Paint to Select mode (see p. 47) or working on a mask... only in this case, it's like using a 3D brush!

At right, a typical first effort: showing how a solid colour layer appears after scrawling in white with a fuzzy brush on the depth map...

So how can you go about creating a depth map? Just activate the layer in the Layers tab and click the **Add Layer Depth Map** button. You'll see a thumbnail of the depth map appear next to the layer name. Initially, the depth map appears solid black, i.e. with zero depth. When you create a depth map, the 3D Effects and 3D Lighting layer effects are switched on by default (so that depth will be visible); the 3D Lighting contributes a bevel effect around the edge, providing initial edge relief. The Colour tab switches to Greyscale mode with White initially the foreground colour and Black the background colour—and you're ready to go!

The basic way to produce an effect is to paint or erase on the depth map. Painting in a lighter shade adds "highs," while painting in a darker shade adds "lows." The fill and selection tools, work, too! For example, instead of starting with an all-black depth map, you can fill all or part of the depth map with grey to start with, and then use painting or eraser tools.

- Try following the steps above and experiment with your own "handwriting" in 3D.

- Try using the Text Tool to create a selection in the shape of text, then paint inside it.

While working on the layer, you can switch back and forth between the image level, depth map, and (optional) mask by clicking the appropriate thumbnail. You can also switch the depth map off and on to assess its contribution to the image, or subtract it for creative reasons: **Shift**-click its preview thumbnail, next to the layer name (when the depth map is switched off a red 'X' appears across the thumbnail).

Bitmap selected   **Depth Map selected**

Once you've understood the basic idea of 3D-by-painting, you might want to try another way of incorporating depth information: create a suitable bitmap image separately (or borrow one from somewhere else) and then paste it via the Clipboard to an existing PhotoPlus depth map. See PhotoPlus help for the details. And needless to say, you can combine depth maps with 3D layer effects or Instant Effects tab presets to create even more fascinating surfaces and textures.

No question about it: these tools will add a whole new dimension to your artwork!

Masks

Masking in a program like PhotoPlus is slightly more complicated than applying masking tape to the screen! But fundamentally the concept is the same: you can hide certain parts of an image—in this case by rendering them transparent, hence invisible. To do that, you create a **mask** on a non-Background layer. You can also use a mask with an adjustment layer, too—to restrict the effect to certain regions.

By changing the greyscale values on the mask (using the paint tools and other devices), you can effect corresponding changes in the opacity of the underlying layer's pixels. For example, by "blacking out" on the mask, you render the layer's underlying pixels transparent, and they disappear from the image.

On an adjustment layer, blacking out hides the adjustment's effect. And because you're working with 256 levels of grey (i.e. opacity), tremendous variations are achievable.

Besides the creative possibilities, ranging from vignetting to multi-layer montage to gradient masking and beyond, a great feature of working on a mask is that it is "temporary"—if you don't like the way things are going, you can abandon your changes and start over without ever having affected the actual pixels on the layer!

Each non-Background layer can have one mask at any given time. (The Background layer can't have one because it doesn't support transparency.) Mask information, like layer information, can only be preserved by saving the image in the native PhotoPlus (.SPP) format.

Mask-making

Here are the three basic steps in using a mask:

1. Create the mask on a layer.

2. Edit the mask itself to "preview" changes to the layer.

3. Merge the mask with the layer to make the changes permanent, or delete the mask without applying changes.

Let's take these in turn. (The description assumes you're working with a standard layer, but the procedures are similar for adjustment layers.)

1 Creating the Mask

Before you can use a mask, you have to create it on a particular layer. The mask can start out as all transparent (revealing the whole layer) or all opaque (hiding the whole layer)—or you can create a mask from a selection, in which case part of the mask will be transparent and the rest opaque.

The choice depends on how you want to work with the layer's contents. By darkening portions of a clear mask, you can selectively fade underlying layer pixels. By lightening an opaque mask, you selectively reveal layer pixels.

To create a mask, first select the layer where you want to create the mask, and select specific region(s) if desired. Choose **Add Mask** from the Layers menu and then one of the following from the submenu:

- **Reveal All** for a transparent mask over the whole layer

- **Hide All** for an opaque mask over the whole layer

- **Reveal Selection** for an opaque mask with transparent "holes" over the selected region(s)

- **Hide Selection** for a transparent mask with opaque "blocks" over the selected region(s)

-

You can also click the layer's **Add Layer Mask** button to create a Reveal All mask (or Reveal Selection if there is one).

 On the Layers tab, a Mask Thumbnail appears (see opposite), confirming that a mask exists, in this case used to produce a vignette effect around the Statue of Liberty.

2 Editing on the Mask

In Edit Mask mode, you can use the full range of painting tools, selection options, and effects to alter the mask's greyscale values. These manipulations cause corresponding changes in opacity, which in turn changes the appearance of the pixels on the layer itself.

Remember, as long as you are editing the mask, you're only seeing a preview of changes on the layer. No permanent changes will be applied until you actually merge the mask with the layer. You can switch out of Edit Mask mode at any time to work directly on the layer (or any other part of the image), then switch back to resume work on the mask.

To edit the active layer's mask, click the Mask Thumbnail, or check **Mask>Edit Mask** on the Layers menu. (Click the layer's bitmap thumbnail or uncheck the menu item to switch out of Edit Mask mode.) The Colour tab switches to Greyscale mode when you're editing a mask, and reverts to the previous setting when you exit Edit Mask mode. This means anything you paste from the Clipboard onto the mask will automatically be converted to greyscale. The image window's titlebar appends "Mask," indicating that a mask is currently being edited.

In Edit Mask mode, you're normally viewing not the mask, but rather the effects of changes "as if" you were making them on the layer below. Adding a Reveal All mask can be a bit confusing, because there's initially no evidence the mask is there at all (i.e. the layer appears exactly the same as it did before you added the mask)! It's sometimes helpful to switch on the **View Mask** setting (**Alt**-click the mask preview thumbnail, or use the Layers menu), which hides the layer and lets you see only the mask, in all its black, white, or greyscale glory. For example, a Reveal All mask appears pure white in View Mask mode. This represents a clear mask with no effect on the underlying pixels' opacity.

View Mask can also be useful in the latter stages of working on a mask, to locate any small regions that may have escaped your attention.

You can **disable** the mask (**Shift**-click the mask preview thumbnail or check **Disable Mask** on the Layers menu) to see how the layer looks without the mask's effects. Note that disabling the mask is not the same as cancelling Edit Mask mode—it only affects your view of the layer, not which plane (i.e., mask or layer) you're working on. When the mask is disabled, a red "X" appears across its thumbnail.

🖗 If you want to fine-tune a mask or layer's position independently of each other it's possible to unlink them. You may have noticed a small link button between the layer and mask thumbnails on the Layers tab, i.e.

A click on this button will unlink the layer and mask, changing the button to display a red cross through it ( ). By selecting the layer or mask thumbnail, you can then drag the layer or mask on the page, respectively. After fine tuning, click the button to relink the mask to the layer.

You can also **create a selection** directly from the mask by selecting its preview thumbnail and choosing **Create from Mask** from the Select menu. Within the resulting selection, pixels that are lighter on the mask (conferring more opacity) become relatively more selected. This correlates with Paint to Select mode (see p. 47), where painting in lighter tones also confers "selectedness."

3 Applying changes to the layer

Once you're satisfied with the appearance of the layer as seen with the mask enabled, you can choose **Mask>Merge Mask** from the Layers menu to make the changes permanent.

Of course, you may choose to **delete** the mask (choose **Mask>Delete Mask** from the Layers menu) without applying changes... perhaps to try again. In either case, whether merged or deleted, the old mask is no longer present and the layer is ready to accept a new mask.

Merging masks reduces clutter and file size, but note that the effects of masking appear in exported images whether or not you've merged masks.

Tutorial Resources

For more experience with the tools and techniques covered in this chapter, we recommend these PDF-based tutorials available from PhotoPlus's Help menu. All involve working with multiple layers:

Try this tutorial...	For practice with these tools and techniques...
Using the Clone Tool	Clone Tool to 'remove' unwanted objects from a photo
Replacing Photo Backgrounds	Extract command to remove the subject from a photo and place it on a different background
Combining Depth Masks with 3D Effects	Depth map fingerprint on a square of "chocolate"
Using Paths	Depth map hand print, using functions on the Paths tab
Creating an Oil Painting Effect	Oil painting effect applied to a photo

Preparing
Web Graphics

One of the main uses for PhotoPlus is to produce graphics for use on the web. This chapter looks at the most popular Web graphics file formats, techniques for creating and editing animations, and two specialized techniques (image slicing and image maps) used to extend the performance of Web images.

"Performance" may seem like an odd aspect of graphic design, but it's actually one of the key factors in designing for the Web. Among other things, it means load time: how long it takes for your photo to display completely in a Web browser. In practice, it's hard to measure. Things like connection bandwidth and server speed all play a part, although less so with the rollout of high-speed home broadband services continuing apace.

The PhotoPlus **Export Optimizer** will greatly help you in reducing file sizes as far as possible while maintaining image quality. For related background material, be sure to consult the "Colour concepts" and "Optimizing images" sections of Chapter 8.

Formats for the Web

Here are some general notes on the principal file formats used for Web pictures and animation—.GIF, .JPG, and .PNG—and details on the options you'll encounter in the PhotoPlus Export Optimizer.

- The details will make a lot more sense if you have the Export Optimizer open. Try using Double or Quad view for side-by-side quality comparisons at different settings.

.GIF format

The .GIF (Graphics Interchange Format) file format is universally supported in Web browsers for both static and animated Web graphics. It's a **lossless** format (there's no image degradation) with excellent compression but a limitation of 256 colours. Use it for non-photographic images with sharp edges and geometrics—for example buttons, bursts, decorative elements, and text graphics. It's suitable for greyscale photos as well.

The .GIF format supports binary transparency. That is, any portion of the image may be either fully opaque or fully transparent. Typically, GIFs use transparency to eliminate the box-shaped frame around the graphic that would otherwise be present. Thus elements with rounded edges, such as characters or shapes, preserve their contours over any background colour or pattern.

The Export Optimizer provides special GIF options that help you preserve semi-transparency if you've employed **antialiasing** or **feathering** in your original image. The .GIF format still wants "all or nothing," but you can opt to **dither** the alpha (transparency) channel and/or select a **matte** colour with which semi-transparent pixels will be smoothly blended. Pixels that aren't 100% transparent will still end up opaque, but the image will look a lot better.

GIF is also a multi-part format, which means one file can store multiple images. As such, it's the preferred format for Web animations.

.JPG format

The **.JPG** or **JPEG** (Joint Photographic Experts Group) file format, like .GIF, is universally supported in Web browsers. Unlike .GIF, it encodes 24-bit images and is a **lossy** format (i.e. it discards some image information) with variable compression settings. JPG is clearly the format of choice for full-colour photographic images. For "black and white" (256-level, 8-bit greyscale) photos, it has no particular advantages over .GIF.

The unique aspect of exporting as a JPG is in fact the slider control you use to choose a Quality setting. At one end of the scale, the export applies maximum compression (0% Quality) and produces an extremely small (but quite ugly) image. At the other end, there is effectively no loss of quality (100%), but file sizes are relatively much larger, although still compact compared to BMPs, for example. When choosing a quality setting for .JPG export, keep in mind the number of times you expect to be re-exporting a particular image.
A photograph may look fine in the Export Optimizer the first time you export it at, e.g. 60% Quality, but after several such saves, you'll really see a quality loss.

PhotoPlus also supports the **JPEG 2000** (.JP2, .J2K) format, which uses wavelet compression and reduces file sizes significantly better than .PNG (see below) but does not support transparency.

.PNG format

For Web graphics, the newer **.PNG** (Portable Network Graphics, pronounced "ping") format has a number of advantages over .GIF—the main ones, from an artist's perspective, being "lossless" 24-bit images and support for variable transparency. Whereas .GIF supports simple binary ("on-off") transparency, .PNG allows up to 254 levels of partial transparency for normal images. The image file includes an "alpha channel" that directs pixels in the foreground image to merge with those in a background image.

Most commonly used with 24-bit images, antialiasing creates the illusion of smooth curves by varying pixel colours—for rounded images that look good against any background, not just against a white background. It's especially useful for the small graphics commonly used on Web pages, such as bullets and fancy text. Because .PNG is lossless and full colour, it's also an excellent storage format for work-in-progress.

Recommended .PNG export settings

Bit Depth: Set a bit depth which reflects the amount of colour in your photo. Enable the smallest bit depth first then increase bit depth values until you arrive at the lowest file size that will preserve an acceptable appearance. If your export does not require transparency, uncheck **Transparent** then try increasing bit depth up to 24 bit (32 bit is always transparent).

Palette: Choose **Optimized** to let the PhotoPlus export filter determine the best colours to apply, but without regard for standard colours. Choose **Web** to reduce the colours to only those found in the 216-colour palette used by Web browsers. This will ensure that an image you place on a Web page won't change its appearance when viewed by users of most other systems or browsers.

Dither: Dithering schemes substitute pixel patterns for original colours to preserve apparent colouration when the actual number of colours in the image is being reduced. Choose **Ordered** (not available for animations) for a more regular dot pattern, and **Error diffusion** for a more adaptive dot pattern.

Matte: Check this option and click the colour sample to choose a colour with which semi-transparent pixels will be smoothly blended.

Transparent: As PNG files support **transparency**, PhotoPlus gives you the option of exporting 1, 2, 4, 8 or 24-bit PNGs with or without a transparent background; 32 bit PNGs are always transparent. Check **Transparent** to turn clear "checkerboard" regions of your graphic (those with 100% transparency, i.e. 0% opacity) into fully transparent regions in the PNG. All other regions will become opaque. If unchecked, transparent regions will become white (or the selected Matte colour). You can also select a dithering method for just the alpha-channel pixels... try each option and see which looks best!

Producing Web Animations

Animation creates an illusion of motion or change by displaying a series of still pictures, rapidly enough to fool the eye—or more accurately, the brain. With PhotoPlus, it's easy to create and edit images with multiple frames, then export them as animated GIFs that a Web browser can play back. You use exactly the same tools and interface as for creating standard, multi-layer PhotoPlus images, with an extra tab window that includes all the additional controls you need to set up frames, add special effects, and preview the animation. Once you're satisfied, use the Export Optimizer to output to the .GIF file format.

The **.GIF** format is what makes Web animation possible, for a couple of reasons. First, it's universally supported by Web browsers. Second, it's a multi-part format, capable of encoding not just one image but multiple images in the same file. A GIF animation player or Web browser can display these images in sequence, in accordance with certain settings (looping, frame delay, etc.) included in the file. The result—it moves!

PhotoPlus gives you the choice of creating your animations from scratch, then exporting to .GIF, starting out by importing a .GIF animation and then editing it, or for existing photos in PhotoPlus, the Animation mode can be entered by selecting **Convert to Animation** from the File menu. Either way, once PhotoPlus detects an animation is required, it switches on the Animation tab. If the image file is new, you'll see a single, blank frame, labelled "Frame 1." If you've imported an animation, the tab displays each frame separately. Animation files can have one layer, or many (see below), but all their layers are standard (transparent) layers; there's no Background layer. (If you need to brush up on the concept of layers, see p. 103.) If a photo is used, the first frame will be the photo image.

Layers and frames

Animations are defined by the **Animation tab** (docked next to the Documents tab at the bottom of your workspace) working together with the **Layers tab**. For an animated GIF of a rotating spiral (SWIRL1.GIF in your PhotoPlus Tutorials/Workspace folder) the Animation tab would display as follows.

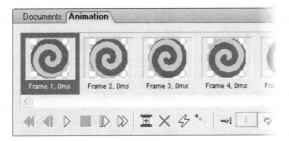

Notice the playback control buttons on the left, below the frames.

- You can click the **Play** button to preview the animation, and click Stop to freeze it. Try the other playback buttons, for first, previous, next, and last frame while you're at it!

Other buttons on the tab offer frame management control of one or more selected frames simultaneously. **Shift**-click or **Ctrl**-click to select adjacent or non-adjacent frames, respectively.

- Use the **New Frame** button to clone selected frames.

- Use the **Delete Frame** button to remove selected frames.

- The **Effects** button applies animation effects to selected frames.

- The **Tween** button, short for "in-betweening", automatically creates a chosen number of frames between the previous or next frame and a currently selected frame—the layer objects are repositioned in each new frame to give a smoother transition of your animation during playback. Opacity and effects can also be tweened as well as object position.

Additional options are available by Right-clicking on any of the frames. The flyout lets you:

- **Reverse Frames,** as it suggests, to reverse the order of selected frames.

- **Flatten Frames** simplify your animation project by flattening all frames (individual frames cannot be flattened). Use to rationalize your layers after animation design.

- **Unify Layer across Frames** to mirror the attributes of a frames' layers to other layers with respect to Position, Opacity, Blend Mode, Visibility and Effects. Select specific or all frames ensuring that the "target" frame which possesses the attribute(s) to be copied is selected last. All "destination" frames adopt the layer attributes of the "target" frame.

- **Add Layer to Each New Frame** which means that each new frame can be edited independently as it occupies its own layer.

Let's examine the Swirl animation more closely. In this file (as in any imported GIF animation) the individual frames each have been assigned one layer in the PhotoPlus image.

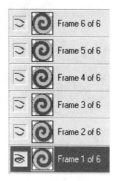

On the Layers tab, the layer stack for this animation corresponds nicely with the frame sequence, with default names—in this case, "Frame 1 of 6" to "Frame 6 of 6."

- Select Frame 1 on the Animation tab.

Notice that on the Layers tab only the "Frame 1" layer is marked as shown, with an open-eye button; the other layers are all hidden, with closed-eye buttons.

- Now select Frame 2 on the Animation tab.

This time, only the "Frame 2" layer will be shown, and the rest will be hidden. And so on with the other frames.

The above example, with its one-to-one correspondence between frames and layers, is easy to grasp but deceptively simple. Don't make the mistake of thinking that a "frame" is just another name for a "layer." Frames in PhotoPlus are actually much more versatile!

Key point: A so-called "frame" is really just a particular state or snapshot of the various layers in the image, in terms of three layer properties:

1   **Shown/Hidden**: Which layers are shown and which are hidden

2   **Position**: The position of the contents of each "shown" layer

3   **Opacity:** The opacity setting of each "shown" layer

As you switch between frames, you are switching between states of the image. In the simple example above, the six frames define six states in terms of Property 1—each of the six frames defines a different layer as "shown." We could rearrange the stacking order of the layers, or rename them—and the animation itself wouldn't change.

Thus, when you create a new frame on the Animation tab, you're not adding a new layer. The new frame merely enables you to define a new state of the layers that already exist. Of course, you *could* go on and create an additional layer, but then all your frames would need to take that layer into account—in other words, hide it when it wasn't needed.

Notes on animation

- In practice, you can use one, two, or even all three of the layer properties when creating a given piece of animation. Just remember that a separate layer is only required for each element that moves independently, or each differently-drawn state of a given element. An element that doesn't change its shape or colour, but merely moves about or changes opacity (appears or disappears), can be animated on a single layer.

- With a little forethought and sketching, you can figure out in advance how many layers you'll need. Then you can set up the image with the right number of layers to begin with.

- To preserve layer properties, be sure to save the image in the native PhotoPlus (.SPP) format. You can reopen an image you've exported as a GIF, but it will have lost PhotoPlus layer properties like opacity and position.

- Although .SPP animations and .SPP pictures share the same file extension, there's no direct conversion option—a file either has animation properties, or it doesn't. To convert an .SPP picture file to an animation, or extract a single frame from an animation to a picture, first create a new image window and then use conventional copy/paste commands to copy elements and/or layers from one file to the other.

- Use animations sparingly on Web pages. Like all attention grabbers, they can lose their impact if overused. Also, animated .GIFs (because of the additional image information) are substantially larger than a static graphics, a consideration if you expect people to view your pages over a slow Internet connection.

- PhotoPlus also lets you export animations to the .AVI movie format (for details, search "AVI" in the online help Index). AVIs are suitable for specialized multimedia work, but are neither compact nor universal enough for general use on Web pages.

Animation effects

The Animation Effects dialog, accessible via the **Effects** button on the Animation tab, lets you turn a variety of PhotoPlus effects into animated transition sequences (see the *Being Creative - Applying special effects* section of the **How To tab** for a visual indication of what each effect can do). The process "in-betweens" or "morphs" a layer from a designated starting frame to some end-state over a specified number of frames, creating one new layer per frame. If you like, you can select a "Ping Pong" option that includes a reverse transition so the final frame looks just like the first one.

To use text or shapes with animation effects, first merge the layer into a standard layer, or convert it to a standard layer by right-clicking on the layer name and choosing **Rasterize** from the menu.

You can either have PhotoPlus create a sequence of new frames for the effect (check **Create as new frames**) or you can create some empty frames yourself and then generate the effect with the **Create as new frames** option unchecked. This will integrate the new layers into the existing blank frames, beginning with the designated Start frame.

Image Slicing

Image slicing and **image maps** are two convenient ways to create navigation bars and clickable graphics for Web pages. With image slicing, a graphic is carved up into smaller graphics—each of which can have its own link, like any Web graphic—and PhotoPlus saves the sections as separate files when you export the image. The process also exports HTML tags describing a table containing the separate graphics, allowing a Web browser to reassemble them seamlessly. The result appears as a single larger graphic, but with different regions linked to different targets.

For example, the menubar graphic (below top)......can be sliced into four separate graphics (below bottom), each linked to a different Web page.

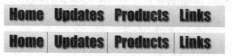

The Image Slice Tool lets you divide the image into sections, which can be exported to the .GIF and .JPG file formats. You can specify alternate text and URL links for each of the image sections individually.

Slicing an image

The **Image Slice Tool** on the Standard toolbar looks like a small, black-handled knife. When it is selected, the cursor also changes to a small knife.

To slice an image horizontally (left to right) select the tool and left-click on the image. **Shift**-click to slice an image vertically (top to bottom). Repeat as many times as necessary. Each click inserts a slice guide. You can move a guide up or down by dragging it, or delete a guide by dragging it out of the image window.

To specify the alternate text and/or URL link for an image slice, right-click it and enter the information into the dialog, then click **OK**.

When exporting a sliced image, check the **Create Image Slices** box on the Export dialog. Specify a name and folder for the files as usual, and choose an either .GIF or .JPG as the export file type.

This will create multiple files in the specified folder, depending on how many slices you have defined. There will be a series of image files (for example, MYFILE0V0.GIF, MYFILE0V1.GIF, etc.) and a single HTML file (for example, MYFILE.HTM). The HTML file contains the tags for the set of image slices, ready to be pasted into the source code for the Web page.

Image Maps

Whereas image slicing subdivides an entire graphic into smaller graphics and exports them separately, image maps consist of **hotspots** that you draw with special tools over selected parts of an image. When a visitor passes their mouse cursor over the hotspot, a small caption is displayed and the pointer will change to a pointing hand. Clicking the mouse while the cursor is over the hotspot will invoke a hyperlink to a specified URL.

You assign each hotspot its own target—for example, the URL of a Web page. Hotspots aren't attached to a particular image, but become part of a larger "map" that gets exported along with an image and turns into HTML code. It's then up to you or your Web developer to embed the image map code properly into the Web page.

Creating image maps by hand can be difficult and time-consuming, but PhotoPlus makes it easy. The **Image Map Tools** flyout on the Standard toolbar displays a flyout menu of tools for creating and editing image maps.

There are four image map tools:

- The  **Image Map Selection** tool, used to modify the area drawn with one of the other tools and to actually set the image map properties;

- The  **Image Map Rectangle** tool, used to draw a rectangular hotspot;

- The  **Image Map Circle** tool, used to draw a circular hotspot;

- The  **Image Map Polygon** tool, used to draw a polygonal hotspot.

Creating hotspots

To begin, click the **Image Map Tools** flyout and choose the rectangle, circle, or polygon tool (shown above). Use the tool to draw a hotspot on the active layer. To draw a polygon, drag and release the mouse button to define each line segment; double-click to close the polygon. Note the turquoise shading that denotes a hotspot.

To edit a hotspot, click the **Image Map Tools** flyout and choose the **Image Map Selection** tool then click on the hotspot. To resize the hotspot, drag from an edge. To move the hotspot, drag from the centre. Right-click the hotspot with the selection tool to delete it, set layer options, or access hotspot properties.

In the Image Map dialog, enter the text which will pop up when the cursor moves over the hotspot, and the full URL for the hotspot to link to. Previously used URLs are saved and can be selected from the drop-down list by clicking on the arrow at the end of the box.

Normally you will export the image for which you have created the image map as a .GIF (for non-photographic images) or a .JPG (for photographic images). We recommend that you use the Export Optimizer (choose **Export Optimizer...** from the File menu) to compare the quality and file size which results from various settings.

Make sure that the **Create HTML for Image Maps** box is checked in the Export dialog, then click **Save**. This will create identically named .HTM and image files. The HTML file contains the tags for the image map, ready to be pasted into the source code for the Web page.

By the way, if you're looking for a powerful yet easy-to-use tool for Web page design, look no further than **Serif WebPlus,** which lets you create your own Web site from scratch or from a vast selection of eye-catching design templates. WebPlus enables effortless, WYSIWYG Web page design—and you can incorporate the animations, sliced images, and image maps you've created with PhotoPlus.

Macros and Batch Processing

Understanding Macros

If there is a command that you want to repeatedly perform in PhotoPlus, you can apply a macro. Put simply, a macro is a saved sequence of commands that can be stored and then recalled at a later date. Macros can be used for:

- Downsampling

- Reformatting

- Applying effects

- Image adjustments

There are hundreds, possibly thousands, of macros that could be recorded for PhotoPlus. The good news is that PhotoPlus already offers an extensive range of pre-recorded macros ready for your use. These macros are available in the **Macros** tab, where they are separated into various categories including Colour, Commands, Effects, and Frames (shown) to name but a few.

Each category is accessible via a drop-down menu. When a new category is selected a scrollable list of macros for that category is made available.

Next to each macro you may have noticed an ▸ icon which, when clicked, displays the commands for the macro. For example, a macro that creates a chrome photo frame would have a series of recorded commands listed chronologically. They may be enabled, disabled, reordered or made interactive "on the fly".

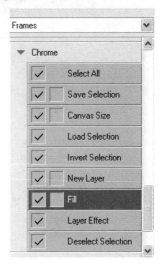

As with many objects within PhotoPlus, you can cut, copy, paste or even duplicate any macro. This allows you to reorganize your macros into different categories.

Recording a Macro

Of course at some point you may want to record your own macro. It's probably a good idea to create a new category into which you can save your newly recorded macros—this keeps them separate from the pre-recorded macros supplied with PhotoPlus. This is because recorded macros will be indistinguishable from your preset macros once recorded.

When recording macros, it can be a good idea to ensure that the Layout Rulers/Grid units in **File>Preferences** are set to "percent". This approach ensures that recorded macro commands such as document resizing or framing are carried out in proportion to the original photo rather than by an absolute value. Imagine adding an absolute frame size to a small photo that would otherwise be acceptable on the larger photo. Obviously, on some occasions you may want to use absolute values—simply use absolute grid units.

Let's look at recording a macro..

- Use the ⌷ **New Category** and ⌷ **New Macro** buttons at the bottom of the Macros tab to provide, firstly, a suitable category name in the dialog, e.g. Borders, and then, secondly, a macro name in advance of you recording your macro. Let's choose "Silver border 50 pixels" as the macro name.

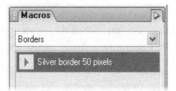

- Make a rough note about what you want to achieve by recording your macro. If you jot down your intended command sequence, your planning will help you make fewer mistakes.

- ◯ Now for some recording! This is possible from within the Macros tab by choosing the **Start Recording** button. Any command you invoke while recording is in progress will be stored.

- Carry out the command sequence you want to record, following the instructions when necessary.

- ⌷ Stop recording your macro with the **Stop Recording** button!

- Click on the macro name, and select the adjacent ▶ icon to view the command list recorded by the macro.

Playing a Macro

To play a macro you need to choose a photo to which you want to apply your recorded or pre-recorded macro. Any macro, whether recorded or pre-recorded, needs to be played to repeat the recorded commands.

- Open the photo you wish to apply the macro to.

- In the Macros tab, select your category from the drop-down list and then your chosen macro by highlighting its name.

- ▷ Choose the **Play** button to play the macro.

Modifying a Macro

It's time to look at the contents of the macro in more detail. We know that when a macro has been recorded the commands are listed under the macro name. So what can we do with this command list? Well it's possible to perform a number of operations—these are described in the following illustration.

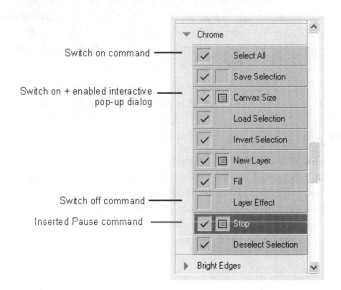

Before going any further, some advice about modifying your macro presets. It's advisable to copy and paste any preset to your own macro category to preserve the integrity of the original macro. This ensures that macros will continue to be of use to you in the future.

By default, macro commands will be enabled (checked) so you are able to disable them if you need to experiment.

With the vast collection of macros and commands at your disposal, it's useful to know that you can copy macros from one category to another easily— simply right-click on the macro to be copied and select **Copy**. You can paste the macro into a new or existing category by right-click then **Paste** (the macro will be added to the end of the category list). Additionally, commands can be moved between macros by drag and drop.

The **Enable\Disable dialog** button allows you to intervene in the macro running process to alter some dialog values while the macro is temporarily "paused". Check the empty box to display a dialog box icon; this will pop-up the appropriate dialog as the macro is run.

Another example of interactivity is the inclusion of a pause into your macro. This allows you to pop up either an instruction or some important notes at pre-defined points as your macro runs. There are a number of reasons for doing this—your macro can't record selections or operations that are particular to each photo so manual selection is essential in some instances, or maybe you want to add a warning to yourself to perform an action (e.g., "try a test export"). Pauses are added after a selected command by right-clicking and selecting **Insert Pause...** from the flyout menu.

It's possible to perform a right-click on any macro or command to **Delete** or **Duplicate** (right-clicking a category also allows renaming). A category currently displayed in the drop-down menu can be edited or deleted via the ▷ **Tab Menu** button at the top right of the tab.

All of the above features provide a high level of control when editing your recorded macro. Try out different combinations of commands to build up your structure. Clearly if you significantly modify your macro command list your macro may become unusable, so it's important to exercise some restraint while editing—experimentation and testing is the rule of thumb. Any changes you make will be applied to the macro such that no file saving is required.

Batch Processing

The batch processing feature is especially useful if you want to repeat the same operation again and again... Batch processing allows you to:

- Specify a source and destination folder as your input and output. There are several advantages to this, mainly that your original photos are not overwritten and that time consuming Save As commands are avoided.

- Bulk convert selected files to a new file type (with different file properties if needed).

- Use a pre-recorded macro as part of the batch process.

- Use a macro you've recorded yourself.

The **Batch** dialog, available from the File menu, is used to perform all of the above operations.

As a pre-requisite, you have to define a specific **Source Folder** for any batch processing operation, whether using a macro or not, or if converting photos to a different file format.

A **Destination** folder can optionally be defined, creating new files in that new location (otherwise the source folder is used).

Using Macros

Macros (see p. 139) can be applied to a batch process easily. Click the **Use Macro** check box and pick a category and macro name. PhotoPlus doesn't differentiate between pre-recorded and recorded macros. If available, they are selected from the same **Category** and **Macro** drop-down menus equally.

Changing File Type

It is possible to convert your photos into one of many different file types available in PhotoPlus. In addition, conversion options such as bit depth, palette, dithering, compression/quality, and matte can be selected in context with each file type.

File conversions can be carried out independently or in conjunction with macros (the dialogs shown opposite apply a frame to all images in c:\ and converts each image to be 32-bit PNG).

Choosing Source and Destination

You may be wondering how batch processing affects your currently loaded photos. PhotoPlus's batch processing only operates on source folder contents and not on the currently loaded photos themselves—so these remain unaffected. However, as a visual check, you will see each photo being converted in the Photo window during batch processing (it's also useful to check the output folder by using Windows Explorer).

Whether you are using macros or not you can select a **Source Folder** and a **Destination Folder** to define which photos are for processing and where you want to save your photos once processed, respectively. To save you time, PhotoPlus will remember previously selected Source and Destination folders while PhotoPlus is loaded.

It is also possible to define a Destination **File Name** for the files to be processed by selecting **Modify....** In the **File Name Format** dialog you can select new file names that can be built up using the current date/time, document names, sequence number, or text string, individually or in combination. Remember to use the sequence number to generate a separate file for every file to be converted—otherwise your first converted file will be overwritten continually.

NOTE: If you don't select a destination folder the source files will be processed and your original files will be overwritten—exercise caution with this option.

Tutorial Resources

For more experience with the tools and techniques covered in this chapter, we recommend the following PDF-based tutorial available from PhotoPlus's Help menu:

Try this tutorial...	For practice with these tools and techniques...
Creating Macros and Batch Processing	Macro basics, Macros tab, Resizing single image, Batch command, Resizing multiple images

Colour and Input/Output Options

This chapter ties together a variety of loose ends... mindful of the fact that every PhotoPlus user will arrive with different needs and prior experience. The other chapters focus on step-by-step procedures to build familiarity with tools and functions. Much of the important theory that underlies the program's workings has had to take a back seat.

As you read through the topics here—all dealing in one way or another with different ways of representing pictures as on-screen bits and bytes—you'll realize how indispensable these underlying concepts are. Although this is the final chapter, it can make a good starting point, too.

Colour Concepts

It's always difficult to draw a line between concepts you should understand before you get started, and those that can wait until you absolutely need them. Here we've collected a few key terms and concepts relating to colour, and presented them roughly in order of priority, trying to keep it simple without oversimplifying. So we suggest you just begin at the beginning, and treat this as a reference section you can revisit at any time.

Bitmaps

First of all, PhotoPlus is all of the following things and more: a "photo editor," a "paint program," a "bitmap editor." It lets you create and manipulate images called "bitmaps," "paint-type" images," or "raster graphics." Don't be overwhelmed by the jargon—all these terms communicate a single concept! **Bitmap** are digital pictures (which may or may not be photographs) represented by lots of coloured dots ("pixels") on a computer screen ("raster"). You create these images by "painting" or filling in regions on the screen, regions that can be as small as a single pixel or as large as the whole screen (or larger).

Bit depth

Technically speaking, a bitmap is basically a "map" of numbers that tell each pixel on a computer monitor what colour it should be. And since computer numbers consist of binary digits (1's and 0's, or "bits"), each pixel in effect has one or more bits backing it up, telling it what to do. From this fact arises the concept of **bit depth** (also known as "pixel depth"), one of the essential attributes of any bitmap image. Bitmaps not only have height and width, they have depth. The more bits assigned to each pixel, the more possible colour states the pixel can be told to take—the greater its "colour depth."

For example: If you're only using 1 bit per pixel, the pixel can only be ON or OFF, in other words "1" or "0," the two states of the bit—hence white or black (**monochrome**). By comparison, a bit depth of 4 bits per pixel can store 16 values; 8 bits per pixel, 256, and so on. 16-bit images have roughly "thousands" of values to describe each pixel's colour, and 24- and 32-bit images have "millions." Not surprisingly, the file size of an image is basically the product of its linear dimensions (number of pixels) times its bit depth, so a picture (perhaps of a heart) saved as a 24-bit image would take up three times as much disk space as an 8-bit version.

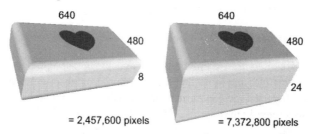

Of course, the appearance of a bitmap on a screen depends not only on the bit depth of the picture but on that of the computer screen displaying it. Just a few years ago (in the "old days"), many monitors were limited to 16 colours, and 256 was a big deal. There were "VGA" and "SVGA," and today the choices include "High Colour" (16 bit) and "True Colour."

Just because you may have a higher-end system, don't forget that many others do not. A 24-bit image with millions of colours may look abysmal on a 256-colour monitor—a key consideration when it comes to creating graphics for the Web, as opposed to CMYK separations for a print publication. In print publishing, designers must worry about whether the colours specified in their electronic images will produce "true" output when reproduced in ink, under standard lighting conditions. In Web or CD-ROM publishing, the main worry is how to **optimize** or reduce the file size as far as possible, while maintaining some semblance of quality in the image (more about optimizing below). Fortunately, PhotoPlus includes tools to support all these needs.

Bit depth in PhotoPlus

One of the main differences between PhotoPlus and most other paint programs is that we've put aside the restrictive notion of working with a limited number of colours. You can work on any image in 24-bit mode, accessing the full colour spectrum via the Colour tab. Native format (.SPP) images are stored in this mode. When and if the time comes to save in a different format, and reduce colours, PhotoPlus provides the Export Optimizer for maximum quality control.

While novices will appreciate the ease of use this approach brings, more experienced users may at first need to adjust to the absence of colour swatches and the constraints of working in 256-colour mode. Still, we're confident that the benefits of concentrating on image production first, and colour reduction last, will soon become apparent!

Tip: You can use the Open dialog to peruse images on your system one at a time, or the Image Browser to display a folder-full of thumbnails at a time. The Open dialog gives the bit depth and dimensions of each image, while the browser shows dimensions (plus additional file data if you right-click a thumbnail and choose **Information...**).

Resolution

Bitmaps are created at a fixed **resolution**, measured in **dpi** (dots per inch) and hence lose quality if resized upwards. Resizing downwards is a different matter, which is why it's always a good idea to scan pictures at higher dpi settings and scale down later (see Tips for Scanning on p. 158). The reproduction quality of bitmaps can vary dramatically, and depends on factors such as the dpi stored in the original file, the dpi used for reproduction (printing), the bit depth, and the scaling factor used in reproduction.

High resolution bitmaps compensate for quality problems, but tend to be very large files.

Colour modes

The PhotoPlus Colour tab includes a control that lets you select one of four **colour modes**: RGB, CMYK, HSL, or Greyscale. You should know something about these modes, even if you only have occasion to work in one or two of them. Much of the terminology overlaps. Let's consider these, starting with the simplest.

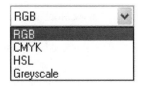

- **RGB** mode is the standard way of describing colours the way they're displayed on computer monitors—as **additive** mixtures of separate Red, Green, and Blue components. Anyone who's seen (in school, perhaps) a demonstration of three projector beams in a dark room, one of each colour, merging to produce a pool of white light, has seen a primitive version of the RGB system. Turn all the elements off and you get black. On computers, 8 bits are used to encode each of the three channels, for a total of 24 bits, and with 256 possible levels (0-255) for each channel. An RGB value of "0,0,0" represents pure black, while a value of "255,255,255" represents pure white.

- **CMYK** is a colour model used for preparing printed work, where ink on paper is the medium that determines colour reproduction. It's based on the **subtractive** principle by which our perception of a pigment's colour depends on which light wavelengths it absorbs and reflects. The four **process inks** are Cyan, Magenta, Yellow, and BlacK (Black is referred to as **Key**). Mix these four inks, and you get black. No ink gives you white (i.e., the colour of the paper)—so if you want white, you must use no ink and let the paper show through! In this subtractive model, the more ink applied, the less light reflected, hence the darker the colour.

  In PhotoPlus, the C, M, Y, and K channel values are given as percentages, from 0 to 100%. PhotoPlus supports CMYK output of process colour separations.

- To understand **HSL**, imagine the difference between watching a TV program on a black and white set as opposed to a colour set. It's the same colour signal, right? But the black and white set doesn't reproduce the colour. What it does pick up is the greyscale or lightness channel of the signal. In the same way, any colour image in PhotoPlus has a channel that stores lightness information. The "L" in HSL stands for **Lightness**. To repeat—and this is important when it comes to understanding topics like masking and blend modes—lightness and greyscale values (and for that matter tones, luminance, and brightness) all refer to the same thing.

  The additional **Hue** and **Saturation** channels in HSL mode together store the colour information that's missing from a simple greyscale image. Like Lightness/Greyscale values, Hue and Saturation channel values are expressed in numbers, ranging from 0 to 255. **Hue** refers to the colour's tint—what most of us think of as rainbow or spectrum colours with name associations, like "blue" or "magenta."

  To understand the HSL colour mode a little better, double-click either the foreground or background colour swatch on the Colour tab and try mixing your own colours using the Adjust Colour dialog. Drag the red button around the outer "wheel", then drag the red button in the inner colour square around. (See PhotoPlus help for details.)

- A **greyscale** image looks like what we would call a "black and white" photograph, which has many levels of black and white (not just two, as in a monochrome line drawing). In PhotoPlus, **Greyscale** mode stores 256 shades of grey or levels of lightness. A value of 0 represents pure black, a value of 255 pure white.

Colour matching

As you might expect from the foregoing descriptions of CMYK and RGB, when it comes to colour reproduction, printing devices and computer screens are on totally different "wavelengths." Printing creates colours by mixing inks which absorb light, while a monitor produces an image by mixing the light itself—as R, G, and B primary colours. The variable brightnesses of each element give the typical computer monitor a range or **gamut** of colours much greater than can be printed with CMYK inks.

The fundamental differences between the CMYK and RGB colour models, and the limited gamut of the printed page compared to the computer screen, create the **colour matching** problem: the challenge of getting your printed output to match what you see in your on-screen design. By calibrating your equipment and using great care, you can achieve a close approximation—but the cardinal rule is "Trust, but verify!" Never simply assume the colours on your screen will turn out exactly the same when printed. It's just very difficult to convert accurately between the two models!

For more accurate results, we strongly recommend that you take advantage of PhotoPlus's colour management features, which let you select ICC device profiles that specify how the internal RGB and/or CMYK colours in your publication's fills and bitmaps will map to on-screen and printed colours. The International Color Consortium (ICC) defines industry standards for converting colour information between various colour spaces and gamuts. Choose **Colour Management...** from the File menu to view a dialog that lets you first of all enable colour management, then select from profiles available on your system. Your monitor or printer manufacturer's Web site should have additional information on how those devices use ICC profiles.

Colour mode tips

- The **Colour Mode** setting (on the Colour tab) determines how image data gets pasted from the Windows Clipboard—in other words, as greyscale values in Greyscale mode, or as full 24-bit colour in any of the other modes.

- If you start editing a layer mask (which represents opacity values by shades of grey), the Colour tab switches temporarily to Greyscale mode. Applying the **Image>Adjust>Greyscale** filter or equivalent adjustment layer, however, doesn't affect the colour mode.

- You can use the Colour Pickup Tool as a probe to read component values in an image. Move the tool around the image and watch the HintLine. Depending on the colour mode, you'll see a readout of values (R, G, B, H, S, L, etc.) under the current cursor position.

Using the Histogram

The Histogram tab is used to view the distribution of colours and tones spread throughout your current selection, selected layer or entire photo (by default). The X-axis shows the colour level (from 0 to 255) and the Y-axis the number of matching colour pixels of that colour level, i.e. the intensity values. A crosshair cursor lets you move around the histogram, displaying the pixel count for the colour level that your cursor is currently placed at. For example, the tab opposite shows the cursor at colour level 55 (visible in the darker region), which has a count of 219 pixels.

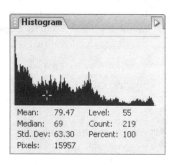

A histogram can be shown for the individual Red, Green or Blue channel, or the composite of the three, the RGB channel (shown). Luminance (or lightness) can also be shown as a histogram.

You can click the ▷ **Tab Menu** button at the top right of the tab to reveal a flyout. To change to a different channel, pick a channel from the list or display statistics (as shown above) by checking **Show Statistics**.

Viewing statistics

With statistics enabled, you can place the cursor at any point on the histogram to view pixel intensity values for composite RGB, each specific colour or luminance level. To view values for a range of colour or luminance levels, hold down your mouse button and drag to select the area for analysis.

The statistics display will show:

- **Mean**—The average intensity value.

- **Median**—The middle value in a range of intensity values.

- **Std Dev.**—Shows how intensity values deviate from normal.

- **Pixels**—Total number of pixels present in the histogram.

- **Level**—Shows intensity level under the mouse cursor.

- **Count**—The total no. of pixels for the intensity level under the mouse cursor.

- **Percent**—The cumulative number of pixels at the selected intensity levels (hold down mouse button and drag), expressed as a percentage of the total number of pixels in the histogram.

By analysing histogram information you can build up an understanding of the colour distribution in your photo, and more importantly any colour deficiencies that may exist.

Optimizing Images

In a perfect world, there would be just one digital picture format that everybody used. Infinite storage capacity and bandwidth would allow full-colour images to be stored and transmitted instantly, uncompressed... but let's leave that for a sci-fi novel! The reality is that at least hundreds of picture formats have been created, with more on the way. A dozen or so are currently in widespread use among computer professionals. The tradeoff between image quality and file size will remain a fact of life. Hence the need to **optimize images**—that is, achieve the best quality in the least file size, and within whatever other constraints (such as number of colours) the job may impose.

PhotoPlus features a powerful **Export Optimizer** (introduced in Chapter 2) that serves as your "command centre" for exporting images to various formats. It not only provides a variety of options for each supported format, but lets you compare image quality using different settings and even retains your preferred settings for each format. You can access the Export Optimizer at any time—not just when exporting—to take advantage of its comparison capabilities. While the visual previews speak for themselves, some of the available settings may need some explanation.

Palettes

The PhotoPlus Export Optimizer offers two standard **Palette** options when you export using 8 bits or less. A colour palette (no relation to a "floating" palette) is a table of colour values that gets stored with any image having 256 colours or less. This could mean a .BMP, .GIF, .PCX, or .WMF image—plus quite a few more. Computer users with high-colour monitors may not give it much thought, but in the realm of 256-colour displays, palettes can make a great deal of difference. Windows itself reserves "slots" for its own "system" colours, and each application must "declare" a palette while the graphics system tries to ensure peaceful coexistence. When several colourful applications are in use, and you switch from one to another, you sometimes see the ghastly result of palettes clashing as neither application wants to relinquish its hold on a scarce system resource.

To avoid that kind of calamity when displaying Web pages, both Netscape and Microsoft browsers use the same **Web-safe** palette of 216 colours to display images. Since you've gotten this far, you may be interested to know that the Web-safe palette is based on *RGB values that are either 0, or divisible by 51.* Permissible values are in the series 0, 51, 102, 153, 204, 255. So, for example, the RGB definition "0,102,51" would be a safe Web colour, while "0,102,52" would not.

If you're exporting at 256 colours or less, and Web display is not an issue, there's no question you should choose the **Optimized** setting—as a quick side-by-side comparison in the preview window will always confirm. The program will always do a better job when it's allowed to select a range of colour values that best match those in the 24-bit version, rather than having to apply the same 216 colours every time.

Note: When you open an image that already has an associated palette, PhotoPlus doesn't attempt to hold on to the palette—it always re-optimizes, even if you use the **Save Original** command. Usually this yields the best possible results; but if keeping exactly the same image palette is essential to your particular application, our advice would be to export from PhotoPlus in 24-bit mode and use a third-party program to apply the palette.

Dithering

Dithering of the digital kind (not to be confused with "showing flustered excitement or fear") comes into play with images being reduced to 256 colours or less. It's a method of approximating colours outside the actual image palette—for example, by alternating pixels of red and blue from within the palette to produce the visual impression of a purple colour that's not in the palette. Applications (including Web browsers) use dithering in 256-colour mode if the images being displayed include colours outside the application palette. This can degrade solid-colour areas and is one of the main reasons to export Web-bound images using the Web-safe palette.

When you're exporting to 256 colours or less, PhotoPlus lets you choose whether or not to use dithering. If you have an image with few colours, and preserving areas of solid colour is essential, you should opt for *no dithering*—and the export filter will pick "nearest-match" colour values from the palette being applied. You may see some colour shifting, but the solid colour areas will be preserved. For photographic images, on the other hand, dithering is clearly the best choice. With the "optimized palette" option, you can choose either **ordered** or **error diffusion** dithering. The former produces a discernibly patterned effect, while the latter tends to average away the patterns for a more natural result.

When exporting to the 256-colour .GIF format, PhotoPlus includes an option that lets you select a method of dithering the alpha (transparency) channel separately from the image's colour information. This produces a kind of scattered "see-through" effect that may improve your results, depending how you intend to use the final image.

Compression

Compression schemes, which apply different algorithms to encode the image information with fewer total bits and bytes, are used in many formats. With some, like .BMP and .TIF, the Export Optimizer gives you a choice of compression scheme. In general, use the default setting unless you know for a fact that some other scheme is called for.

The .JPG format, widely used for photographs (and detailed in Chapter 6), is unusual in that you can set the level of quality desired using a slider. As you might expect, the highest-quality setting uses least compression, with no loss of image quality but the largest file size. The lowest-quality setting applies maximum compression for smallest size, but yields rather poor quality. With the aid of the Export Optimizer, you can judge for yourself—but another factor to keep in mind is the number of times you expect to be re-exporting a particular image. A photograph may look fine the first time you export it at a JPG level of 60%, but after several such saves, you'll really see the quality loss. As a rule, keep images in the native .SPP format, or export them using only lossless compression schemes, until it's time for the final export.

File Formats

PhotoPlus can import and export most types of graphics file which you're likely to encounter. In order to use PhotoPlus images in other programs, you will have to export them into one of the widely used formats.

For pictures and animations intended for use on the web, the two prevalent formats are .GIF (for both) and .JPG (just for photos). A newer format, .PNG, affords excellent compression and variable transparency but older browsers may not support it. See Chapter 6 for details on these Web format features and options. (PhotoPlus also lets you export animations to the .AVI movie format.)

For print use, we recommend that you use .TIF or .BMP as most other programs allow you to import files in that format.

If you're exporting an image so that it can be used in four-colour process printing, be sure to enable the CMYK option in the Export Optimizer. The other export formats use the RGB colour model (see p. 151), which is not suitable for use in process printing.

The .WMF metafile format used by Windows can include bitmap data, vector data, or both (in vector images the picture is stored compactly as a set of lines). To generate vector information for scalable images you can work with in a draw program, choose the **Autotraced Metafile** export option. PhotoPlus processes the image and includes traced vector data in the output file.

Tips for Scanning

Scanning hardware and software varies considerably. One myth is that the higher the resolution of your scanner, the better results you'll achieve. While that's true in theory, the real limit to quality is how the image will ultimately be reproduced. Will it end up on the printed page or on-screen? Either way, the real issue is how many "extra pixels" you'll need in the original scan.

If the image will be professionally printed, will that be onto a sheet of newsprint or a glossy coated stock? Paper itself puts a ceiling on reproduction quality. Lower-grade paper tends to spread ink around more easily, so the dots of ink used to print a picture need to be larger. This means a wider **halftone screen** with fewer **lines per inch** (lpi).

If you'll generate your output on a desktop printer, the device will be putting bits of toner or droplets of ink on the paper. On a laser printer, shades of grey result from variations in toner coverage. Desktop colour printers create colour by laying down dots of cyan, magenta, yellow, and black ink. Again, printer resolution and paper type are quite variable. Dpi (**dots per inch**) is the most common measure of print quality. But the lines per inch, based on halftone reproduction, is equally useful. A print resolution of 600 dpi corresponds to about 100 lpi.

- As a general rule, the optimal scanning resolution for print work (in dpi) is about one-third the dpi setting (i.e. twice the resultant lpi) on the printer or other device that will be used. 200 dpi scanning is fine for most printed output.

Or will your image end up on-screen instead of in print? If so, it will no doubt be viewed at standard **screen resolution** of 96 dpi. (That's why this is the default resolution in PhotoPlus.) If you're producing Web images, it makes more sense to regard resolution as a fixed factor, and think in terms of image dimensions instead.

This means that, for an image that will end up on a Web page, it's just possible you can get great results scanning at 100dpi, at exactly the screen dimensions you need. But that's cutting it close, especially if you'll be editing the image at all.

For either print or screen images, you must always take into account what kinds of manipulations you plan to carry out on the image in your photo editor, i.e. PhotoPlus. Colour adjustments, resizing (with resampling), blurring, and other effects tend to disturb the arrangement of pixels in the original scanned image. So let's add another guideline:

- If preserving detail is a consideration—as it almost always is—and you plan to manipulate the image, then give yourself enough pixels to work with! Scan at a higher resolution (or higher size) and scale the image down later.

Of course, file size and the capacity of your system are also factors in choosing scanner settings. It makes little sense to work slowly on a 20MB file, if you'd get the same final quality working quickly with a 5MB file.

Depending on your scanner software, your may be able to perform initial adjustments right at the source. For example, you can use the controls to get a true black on one end and true white on the other. Often you can **de-screen** images to eliminate possible **moiré patterns** (interference between the regular dot patterns in printed images and the scanner's path).

- If your scanner software doesn't provide de-screening, try using the PhotoPlus Gaussian Blur filter to remove moiré. Make sure you've scanned at higher resolution (or size) so that you can then scale down the image to regain detail.

Some other tips:

- If you're scanning a number of pictures, you may find it's faster to save scanned images to disk rather than bringing them directly into PhotoPlus.

- In PhotoPlus, you can use the ⌨ **Straighten Tool** on the Tools Toolbar's Crop flyout to correct for any misalignment in the scan, then perform a crop to reset edges to horizontal and vertical. Use the range of image adjustments to subsequently improve image quality (see p. 56).

EXIF Information

Exchangeable Image File (EXIF) information may be appended to any photo obtained via digital photography. This information relates to picture taking conditions and your digital camera specification.

It is possible to read the EXIF information for any digital photo from **File>Exif Info...**

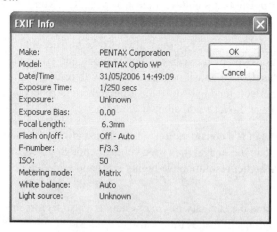

Advanced Printing

In Chapter 2, we dealt with basic single-image printing via the Print dialog's General tab. Now it's time to take a look at the range of advanced printing options PhotoPlus affords.

Positioning, scaling, and tiling

Select the Print dialog's **Layout** tab to specify positioning, scaling, and tiling options.

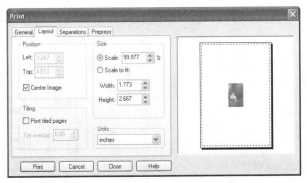

If you uncheck **Centre image**, you can specify the absolute position of the top-left corner of the image. To print at actual size, select **Scale** and choose "100%." To print at a larger or smaller size, choose or type a different percentage value in the list. You can also **Scale to fit** a particular dimensional area or specify the exact **Width** and/or **Height**.

Selecting **Print tiled pages** lets you print oversized artwork on several sheets of paper. Each section or tile is printed on a single sheet of paper; the sheets can then be joined to form the complete page. This option is used for printing at larger sizes than the maximum paper size of your printer (e.g. for posters). To simplify arrangement of the tiles and to allow for printer margins, you can specify a **Tile overlap** value.

The Preview area shows where on the page the image will be printed. It changes according to whether the printer driver is set to portrait (wide) or landscape (tall) orientation.

After specifying options, click one of the other tabs to set more options, or click **Print** to proceed with printing (or **Cancel** to abandon changes).

CMYK colour separations

An offset press needs one independent plate for each colour that will print on the job. PhotoPlus will let you choose to print either a composite copy or colour separations which are used when printing the job to an imagesetter or platesetter.

If the job is created properly, you then get, for each page, one complete negative for each colour. If you were working on a flyer, you could print out a composite copy on your laser or ink jet printer which would give you one piece of paper with the whole flyer, or seps, which would give you four sheets of paper.

The **Separations** tab controls the printing of colour separations.

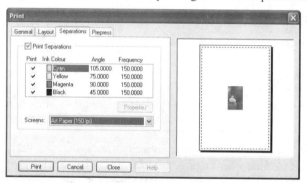

If you are using a PostScript® output device, checking the **Print Separations** box on the Separations tab allows you to choose whether to print separations for process printing and if selected, which separations to print. This box will be greyed out if you are not using a PostScript printer driver.

Normally, separations are not enabled. On a colour printer (e.g. an ink jet), if separations are not enabled you will get a single composite colour page and on a mono printer (e.g. a laser printer) it will give a single greyscale page.

After specifying options, click one of the other tabs to set more options, or click **Print** to proceed with printing (or **Cancel** to abandon changes).

Including printer marks

On the **Prepress** tab, you can specify whether to print various marks as well as the image.

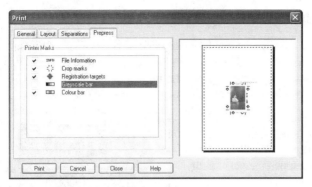

Marks and file information can only be printed if the physical paper size is one inch or more larger all round than the image.

After specifying options, click one of the other tabs to set more options, or click **Print** to proceed with printing (or **Cancel** to abandon changes).

Multi-Image Printing

The last time we checked, photo-quality printer paper was still an expensive commodity! **Multi-image printing** in PhotoPlus lets you conserve this precious resource by "ganging" several images onto a single output sheet—choose **Print Multiple...** on the File menu to get started.

There's no need for complex calculations... in Automatic mode, simply choose a grid template, then drag and drop open images into the cells on the preview page. Other layout options include various Fit commands to expedite image placement; Manual mode, which dispenses with the grid and lets you place images anywhere; and Edit mode, which lets you design your own templates. Once you've placed images into a layout, you can move, resize, rotate or flip them— and of course, print out your page!

Online help provides complete details on the various buttons and functions.

Publishing a PDF File

PDF (Portable Document Format) is a cross-platform file format developed by Adobe. In a relatively short time, PDF has evolved into a worldwide standard for document distribution which works equally well for electronic or paper publishing. PDF documents are uniformly supported in the Windows, Macintosh, and UNIX® environments. Anyone with the free Adobe Acrobat® Reader can view or print out PDF files, either from within a Web browser window or directly—for example, when delivered over a network or on CD-ROM. PDF documents are compact—one-fifth the size of comparable HTML files—for faster transmission.

PDF works well as a medium for distributing standalone files. By letting people download an online PDF file, you can save yourself the trouble and expense of printing multiple copies! PDF is also used extensively for delivering files to professional printers. In recent years, print shops are moving toward the newer **PDF/X** formats—more reliable than PostScript and expressly targeted for graphic arts and high quality reproduction. Several different "flavours" of PDF/X exist; PhotoPlus supports PDF/X-1 and PDF/X-1a.

To export a PhotoPlus picture as a PDF, choose **Publish as PDF...** from the File menu) to display the **Publish PDF** dialog.

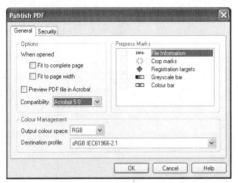

Set basic output options on the dialog's General tab. If handing off a file to a professional printer, choose either "PDF X/1" or "PDF X/1a" in the **Compatibility** list as advised by your print partner. In the Colour Management section, the **Output colour space** setting should always be "CMYK" for professional printing. Select the **Destination profile** recommended by your print partner. Checking **Preview PDF file in Acrobat** automatically opens the PDF in Acrobat after it's been created, so you can review it immediately. (If anything looks amiss, you'll need to fix the problems in the file and regenerate the PDF.)

The Security tab lets you add password protection to keep the contents of your document away from unintended eyes. You can also lock certain capabilities to prevent unauthorized dissemination or changes. For example, you can specify **No document printing** to prevent paper reproduction of the publication's contents, or **No content copying** to help ensure your text can't be easily duplicated somewhere else. You can even enter a master password to give you—and only you—the right to alter these security settings. (Just be sure to remember your password!)

Tutorial Resources

For more experience with the tools and techniques covered in this chapter, we recommend these PDF-based tutorials available from PhotoPlus's Help menu:

Try this tutorial...	For practice with these tools and techniques...
Exploring Colour Spaces	Colour modes: RGB and HSL
Image Formats	Choices in the Export Optimizer

PhotoPlus Keyboard Shortcuts

Tool shortcuts

Press...			With...	To...
Shift	—	—	Selection tools	Add to current selection
	Alt	—	Selection tools	Subtract from current selection
		Ctrl	Selection tools	Move selection contents
	Alt	—	Move Tool	Duplicate selection contents
		Ctrl	Adjustable Selection tools, Crop Tool, QuickShape tools, Image Map rectangle	Constrain aspect ratio when dragging to define shape or region
Shift			Straight Outline Tool	Constrain to 15° angle intervals
	Alt	—	Text, Paintbrush, Airbrush, Fill, Outline, QuickShape tools	Left-click to pick up foreground colour; right-click to pick up background colour
Shift	—	—	Deform tool, Deform Mesh tool, Shape Edit Tool	Drag corner handle to resize relative to fixed point with constrained aspect ratio or rotate at 15° angle intervals
Shift	—	—	as above	Drag corner handle to constrain aspect ratio
	Alt	—	as above	Drag corner handle to resize (unconstrained) relative to fixed point
Shift		Ctrl	as above	Drag corner handle to skew along selection edge
Shift	Alt	—	as above	Drag corner handle to resize relative to fixed point while constraining aspect ratio

	Alt	**Ctrl**	as above	Drag a corner handle to skew constrained relative to fixed point
		Ctrl	as above	Drag corner handle to skew freely
Shift	**Alt**	**Ctrl**	as above	Drag corner handle to change perspective

Menu command shortcuts

Press...		With...	To...
	Ctrl	**Z**	Undo last action
	Ctrl	**Y**	Redo last undone action
	Ctrl	**C**	Copy selection or layer to Clipboard
Shift	**Ctrl**	**C**	Copy merged (all layers as one) to Clipboard
Shift	**Ctrl**	**L**	Paste from Clipboard into selection
	Ctrl	**V**	Paste from Clipboard as new image
	Ctrl	**L**	Paste from Clipboard as new layer
	Ctrl	**+**	Zoom in
	Ctrl	**−**	Zoom out
	Ctrl	**0**	Zoom to Fit
	Ctrl	**[**	Move Layer Up
	Ctrl	**]**	Move Layer Down
	Ctrl	**G**	Group Layers
Shift	**Ctrl**	**G**	Ungroup Layers
	Ctrl	**J**	New Layer from Selection Copy
Shift	**Ctrl**	**J**	New Layer from Selection Cut
	Ctrl	**K**	Link Layers
Shift	**Ctrl**	**K**	Unlink Layers
	Alt	**[**	Select layer above

	Alt	**]**	Select layer below
		Ctrl **E**	Applies last effect
Shift	**Ctrl**	**B**	Show Image Adjustment Colour Balance
Shift	**Ctrl**	**E**	Show Image Adjustment Levels
Shift	**Ctrl**	**H**	Show Image Adjustment Hue/Saturation/Light
Shift	**Ctrl**	**U**	Show Image Adjustment Curves
	Ctrl	**D**	Deselect pixels (select nothing)
	Ctrl	**A**	Select all
	Ctrl	**A**	Cut selection to Clipboard
Shift	**Ctrl**	**D**	Reselect
Shift	**Ctrl**	**I**	Invert selection
	Ctrl	**B**	Load Image Browser
	Ctrl	**M**	Switch on/off grid
	Ctrl	**Q**	Switch on/off guides
	Ctrl	**R**	Switch on/off rulers
	Ctrl	**N**	New image
	Ctrl	**O**	Open file
	Ctrl	**P**	Print
	Ctrl	**S**	Save
	Ctrl	**F4**	Close current image window
	Alt	**F4**	Exit PhotoPlus

Index

2D layer effects, 112
3D layer effects, 112, 113
Add Mask command, 118
Adjust Colour dialog, 74
Adjustable Selection tools, 43
adjustment layers, 58, 117
adjustments
    AutoContrast, 56, 59
    AutoLevels, 56, 59
    Brightness/Contrast, 56, 59
    Channel Mixer, 57
    Colour Balance, 56
    Curves, 56
    Equalize, 57
    Gradient Map, 57
    Greyscale, 57
    Hue/Saturation/Lightness, 57
    Lens Filter, 57
    Levels, 56, 59
    Negative Image, 57
    Posterize, 57
    Replace Colour, 57
    Selective Colour, 57
    Shadow/Highlight/Midtone, 56
    Threshold, 57
Airbrush property, 78
aligning layers and shapes, 87, 107
animation
    .GIF format for Web, 126, 128
    creating, 128
    effects, 132
Animation tab, 27, 128
antialiasing, 44, 75, 88, 91, 98, 126
arrow
    drawing, 87
    selecting shape, 43
artistic filters, 67, See effects
AutoContrast, 56, 59
AutoLevels, 56, 59
autotraced metafile, 158
Average Colour, 65
AVI file format, 131
background colour, 18, 73, 82, 116
Background Eraser Tool, 82
Background layer. See layers
Batch dialog, 143

Batch processing, 143
bit depth, 149
bitmap, 149
blend modes, 77, 104, 110, 113, 114,
    152
blend ranges, 111
blur filters. See effects
Blur Tool, 61
box, drawing, 87
Brightness/Contrast (adjustment), 56, 59,
    63
Brush Options, 79
Brush Tip tab, 24, 76
brush tips, creating custom, 77
Bump Map (layer effect), 114
Burn Tool, 61
cameras, digital
    importing from, 31
canvas, resizing, 17, 49
capturing
    screens, 32
Channel Mixer (adjustment), 57
Channels, 54
Channels tab, 26
Character tab, 27, 99
Chromatic Aberration Remover, 63
circle
    drawing, 87
    placing hotspot, 134
    selecting shape, 43
Clipboard operations, 49, 108, 153
Clone Tool, 84
CMYK
    colour separations, 162
    mode, 74, 152
Colour Balance (adjustment), 56, 63
Colour Management, 153, 165
Colour Pickup Tool, 74, 154
Colour Selection Tool, 44
Colour tab, 18, 24, 73
colours
    adjusting, 56
    choosing, 74
    colour matching, 153
    key colours in gradient, 94
    modes, 74, 151

palettes, 156
replacing, 57
selecting, 44
    tolerance in, 44
separations, 162
storing, 74
theory, 149
Windows system, 156
combination buttons
    for lines, 86
    for paths, 96
    for selection, 45
    for shapes, 86
compression, 125, 157
Conical (gradient fill type), 92
Context Help button, 75
Context toolbar, 17, 23, 24, 29, 45, 52, 60, 61, 76, 82, 83, 88, 90, 91, 93
contrast, adjusting, 56, 59
Copy command, 49
correction
    of images, 60
Create HTML for Image Maps setting, 134
Create Image Slices setting, 133
Crop to Selection command, 50
Crop Tool, 49
cropping, 49, 63
Curved Outline Tool, 89
Curves (adjustment), 56
custom filters, 65
Cut command, 49
Deform Tool, 51
Delete command, 49
Delete Mask command, 120
depth maps, 115
Deselect command, 46
device profiles, 153
diameter (of brush), 77
digital camera (TWAIN) input, 31
Disable Mask command, 119
distortion filters. See effects
distributing layers and shapes, 87, 107
dithering, 127, 157
documents
    sharing by email, 37
Documents tab, 28, 32
Dodge Tool, 61
dpi (dots per inch), 151, 159

drag and drop, 31
drawing. See also tools
    hotspots (image maps), 133
    lines, 75, 88
    shapes, 87
Drop Shadow effect, 113
Duplicate command, 31
Duplicate Layer command, 105
duplicating a selection, 48
edge filters. See effects
Edit Mask mode, 119
Edit tools, 89, 96
effects, 65
    artistic, 67
    blur, 65
        Depth of Field, 65
    distortion, 65
    edge, 65
    emboss, 65
    Gaussian Blur, 160
    Median, 65
    mosaic, 65
    noise, 65
    Paper Cutouts, 65
    render, 65
    Unsharp Mask, 65
Elastic Warp Tool, 83
ellipse
    drawing, 87
    selecting shape, 43
email
    sharing documents by, 37
Equalize (adjustment), 57
Eraser tools, 82
Exif, 160
Export Optimizer, 20, 34, 155
exporting files, 20, 34
    image maps, 134
    image slices, 133
    optimization, 155
Extract command, 44, 112
feathering, 47, 126
features, key, 7
file formats
    .AVI, 131
    .GIF, 125
    .JPG, 126
    .PNG, 126
    .SPP, 20, 34, 104, 117, 131, 150

.WMF, 158
  for Web graphics, 125
Fill command, 90
Fill tools
  Flood, 90
  Gradient, 90
fills
  gradient, 92
    editing, 94
  pattern, 92
  solid, 91
  tolerance in, 91
Filter Gallery, 65
filters. *See* effects or adjustments
  custom, 65
  plug-in, 29
flattening an image, 109
Flip command, 50
Flood Eraser Tool, 82
Flood Fill Tool, 90
foreground colour, 18, 73, 75, 78, 87, 91,
  93, 116
formatting text, 98
frames (animation), 130
Freehand Outline Tool, 88
Gaussian Blur (effect), 160
GIF file format, 125
Gradient Fill Tool, 90
Gradient Map (adjustment), 57
Greyscale (adjustment), 57, 63
Greyscale mode, 74, 116, 119, 152, 153
Grow Selection command, 46
guides, 76
halftone screen, 159
hardness (of brush), 77
heart, selecting shape, 43
HintLine, 51, 154
Histogram, 154
Histogram tab, 25
History tab, 25
hotspots (for image maps), 133
How To tab, 27
HSL mode, 74, 152
HTML
  for image maps, 134
  for image slices, 133
hue, defined, 152
Hue/Saturation/Lightness (adjustment),
  57

hyperlinks
  for image maps, 134
  for image slices, 132
ICC device profiles, 153
Image Browser, 31
image formats. *See* file formats
Image Map tools, 133
Image Slice Tool, 132
importing from TWAIN source, 31
installation, 12
Instant Artist, 67
Instant Effects tab, 25, 113
Invert Selection command, 46
JPEG (.JPG) file format, 126
key colours, 94
keyboard shortcuts, 167
layers, 18, 103
  active, 19, 105
  adjustment, 58, 117
  aligning, 107
  and animation frames, 130, 131
  arranging, 108
  Background, 18, 31, 48, 50, 73, 82,
    93, 103, 104, 105, 108, 110, 112,
    117
  blend modes, 110
  Clipboard operations, 108
  copying, 108
  creating, 105
  cutting, 108
  deleting, 105
  depth maps, 115
  distributing, 107
  duplicating, 105
  extracting parts of, 112
  grouping, 109
  hiding and showing, 106
  layer effects, 68, 112
  linking and unlinking, 107
  merging, 109
  moving, 107
  opacity, 50, 130
  pasting, 108
  Promote to Layer, 50, 105
  selecting all, 107
  selecting linked, 107
  shape layers, 19, 86, 90
  standard layers, 19, 103
  text, 90, 98

text layers, 19
Layers tab, 26, 103, 108, 128
Lens Distortion (correction), 63
Lens Filter (adjustment), 57
Lens Vignette (correction), 63
Levels (adjustment), 56, 59
lighting (render) filters. *See* effects
lightness
    adjusting, 57
    defined, 152
Linear (gradient fill type), 92
Link Layers command, 107
lpi (lines per inch), 159
macros
    modifying, 141
    playing, 141
    recording, 140
Macros tab, 26, 139
manipulating photos, 41
marquee, 18, 42, 43, 45, 47, 49, 50, 76, 97
masking, 117
matte (export option), 36, 126
Median, 65
Merge All command, 109
Merge command (layers), 109
Merge Layer Group command, 110
Merge Mask command, 120
Merge Selected Layers command, 109
Mesh Warp Tool, 52
metafiles, 158
moiré patterns, 160
monochrome, 152
Move Marquee cursor, 45, 48
Move Tool, 48, 107
multi-image printing, 164
navigating
    documents, 32
Navigator tab, 25, 30
Negative Image (adjustment), 57
New Layer Group command, 109
Node Edit Tool, 90
noise filters. *See* effects
opacity, 19, 50, 77, 78, 82, 94, 104, 120, 130
opening an existing file, 30
optimizing images, 155
Outline tools, 85, 96
oval, drawing, 87

Paint to Select mode, 47
Paintbrush Tool, 75
painting. *See* tools
palette, Web-safe, 127, 156
palettes, 74
    colour, 127
palettes, colour, 156
Pan Tool, 30
panning, 30
    all windows, 30
Paste command, 49, 99
paths, 95
Paths tab, 26, 96
Pattern Brush Tool, 80
pattern fill, 92
Pattern Map (layer effect), 114
PDF publishing, 164
pen (input device), 79
Pencil Tool, 79
Photo Studio toolbar, 24, 62, 65, 67, 112
PhotoPlus
    .SPP file format, 20, 34, 96, 104, 117, 131, 150
    key concepts, 17
    key features, 7
    shortcuts, 167
Photoshop .PSD format, 20, 31
Picture Brush Tool, 81
picture tubes (Paint Shop Pro), 77, 81
pie, selecting shape, 43
Pinch/Punch tools, 83
Ping Pong (animation), 132
pixels, 17, 44, 48, 60, 91, 104, 149, 154
plug-in filters, 29
PNG file format, 126
polygon
    drawing, 87
    placing hotspot, 134
Posterize (adjustment), 57
preferences, setting, 29, 41
Print Multiple, 164
printing
    advanced, 161
    basic, 36
    cropping to print sizes, 50
    marks for, 162
    multi-image, 164
    scaling output, 161
    tiling, 161

process inks (CMYK), 152
profiles (device), 153
Promote to Layer command, 50, 105
properties, setting for tools, 29
PSD file format, 20, 31
Publish as PDF, 165
quality
    adjustments for, 160
    in exported images, 125
QuickFix Studio, 62
QuickShape tools, 85, 87, 96
Radial (gradient fill type), 92
raster, 85
Rasterize command, 87, 99, 132
rectangle
    drawing, 87
    placing hotspot, 134
    selecting shape, 43
red eye
    fixing, 60, 63
registration, 12
render filters. *See* effects
Replace Colour (adjustment), 57
Replace Colour Tool, 61
resizing, 17, 49
resolution, 151, 159
retouching, 60
Revert command, 31
RGB mode, 74, 151
Rotate command, 50
saturation
    adjusting, 57
saving files, 20, 34, 156
Scale to fit option, 161
scaling, 161
scanning, 31, 158
Scratch Remover Tool, 61
Screen capture, 32
security options (PDF), 165
Select All Layers command, 107
Select Linked Layers command, 107
Select Similar command, 46
selection, 18, 41
    creating, 41
    deforming, 52
    deselecting, 46
    duplicating, 48
    from mask, 120
    inverting, 46

modifying, 45
Paint to Select mode, 47
resizing, 51
rotating, 51
Text Selection Tool, 99
to and from path, 96
transforming, 52
variable, 47
Selection Deform Tool, 52
Selective Colour (adjustment), 57
Send command, 37
separations, CMYK colour, 162
Shadow/Highlight/Midtone
    (adjustment), 56
Shape Edit Tool, 89
shape layers, 86, 90
shapes
    aligning, 87
    distributing, 87
Sharpen Tool, 61
sharpening, 63
shortcuts, table of, 167
Smudge Tool, 60
Snapping, 42, 48
Solid (fill type), 92
special effects filters. *See* effects
spiral, selecting shape, 43
Sponge Tool, 61
SPP file format, 20, 34, 96, 104, 117,
    131, 150
square
    drawing, 87
    selecting shape, 43
Square (gradient fill type), 92
Standard Selection tools, 42, 50
Standard toolbar, 24
star
    drawing, 87
    selecting shape, 43
Starting PhotoPlus, 21
Startup Wizard, 21
Statistics
    in Histograms, 154
Straight Outline Tool, 88
Straighten Tool, 51
straightening (correction), 63
stroking a path, 96
stylus (input device), 79
support, technical, 12

Swatches tab, 27, 74
system requirements, 12
tab windows, 17
tablet (input device), 79
tabs
    Animation, 27, 128
    Brush Tip, 24, 76
    Channels, 26
    Character, 27, 99
    Colour, 18, 24, 73
    docking and undocking, 23
    Documents, 28, 32
    Histogram, 25
    History, 25, 41
    How To, 27
    Instant Effects, 25, 113
    Layers, 26, 103, 108, 128
    Macros, 26, 139
    Navigator, 25, 30
    Paths, 26, 96
    saving layout of, 28
    Swatches, 27, 74
technical support, 12
text
    adding, 98
    creating selection in shape of, 99
    editing, 98
    layers, 90
text layers, 98
Text Selection Tool, 99
Text Tool, 98
Texture attribute (Brush Options, 79
Thick/Thin Warp Tool, 83
Threshold (adjustment), 57
Threshold command, 47
tiling, 161
toolbars
    Context, 24, 45, 52, 60, 61, 76, 82,
        83, 88, 90, 91, 93
    Photo Studio, 24, 62, 65, 67, 112
    Standard, 24
    Tools, 17, 24
tools, 17
    Adjustable Selection tools, 43
    Blur Tool, 61
    Burn Tool, 61
    Clone Tool, 84
    Colour Pickup Tool, 74, 154
    Colour Selection Tool, 44

Crop Tool, 49
Curved Outline Tool, 89
Deform Tool, 51
Dodge Tool, 61
Eraser tools, 82
Flood Fill Tool, 90
Freehand Outline Tool, 88
Gradient Fill Tool, 90
Image Map tools, 133
Image Slice Tool, 132
Mesh Warp Tool, 52
Move Tool, 48, 107
Node Edit Tool, 90
Paintbrush Tool, 75
Pan Tool, 30
Pattern Brush Tool, 80
Pencil Tool, 79
Picture Brush Tool, 81
Red Eye Tool, 60
Replace Colour Tool, 61
Scratch Remover Tool, 61
Selection Deform Tool, 52
Shape Edit Tool, 89
Sharpen Tool, 61
Smudge Tool, 60
Sponge Tool, 61
Standard Selection tools, 42, 50
Straight Outline Tool, 88
Straighten Tool, 51
Text Selection Tool, 99
Text Tool, 98
Warp tools, 83
Zoom Tool, 29
Tools toolbar, 17, 24
transparency. *See* opacity
    in exported images, 125, 126
TWAIN input, 31
tweening, 129
Twirl tools, 83
Undo options, 41, 83
Unlink Layers command, 107
Unsharp Mask, 65
URLs
    for image maps, 134
    for image slices, 132
Use All Layers command, 104
vector, 85
View Mask setting, 119
Warp tools, 83

wave, selecting shape, 43
Web images
    animations, 128
    file formats for, 125
    performance issues, 125
    Web-safe palette, 127, 156

weight (line thickness), 88
Windows system colours, 156
WMF file format, 158
Zoom Tool, 29
zooming, 30
    all windows, 30